Christian Ethics and
Human Nature

Christian Ethics and Human Nature

Terence Penelhum

The 1999 Diocese of British Columbia
John Albert Hall Lectures
at the
Centre for Studies in Religion and Society
in the University of Victoria

scm press

Copyright © Terence Penelhum 2000

0 334 02812 4

This edition first published 2000 by
SCM Press,
9–17 St Albans Place London N1 0NX

SCM Press is a division of
SCM-Canterbury Press Ltd

Typeset by Regent Typesetting, London
and printed in Great Britain by
Biddles Ltd, Guildford and King's Lynn

THE JOHN ALBERT HALL LECTURES

Churchman, chemist, pioneer, soldier, businessman and philanthropist, John Albert Hall (1869–1933) emigrated from Britain to Canada in the last decade of the nineteenth century and made his home in Victoria, British Columbia. He left a legacy to the Diocese of British Columbia to found a lectureship to stimulate harmony between the Christian religion and contemporary thought. Colonel Hall's generosity sustained the work of three successive Canon Lecturers: Michael Coleman, Hilary Butler and Thomas Bailey. It also helped found the Greater Victoria Lay School of Theology. Since 1995 it has been supporting the lectureship's partnership between the Diocese of British Columbia and the University of Victoria's Centre for Studies in Religion and Society.

The Centre was established in 1991 to foster the scholarly study of religion in relation to the sciences, ethics, social and economic development, and other aspects of culture. As Cosponsor of the John Albert Hall Lecture Series it assists in the fulfilment of the terms of the trust.

John Albert Hall lecturers are outstanding Christian theologians who address themselves to the church, the university and the community during a two-week Fellowship in Victoria, Canada. Publication of these lectures allows a wider audience to benefit from both the lecture series and the work of the Centre.

Contents

Preface

This book contains the four John Albert Hall lectures which I delivered in Victoria, British Columbia, in October 1999. I must begin by thanking all those who helped make this visit to Victoria such an idyllically happy one for my wife and myself, particularly Michael and Anita Hadley, John and Mary Wright, and Alan and Lois Batten. I have given many lectures in the last fifty years, but never in such pleasant circumstances. I also want to thank Harold Coward for the honour of the original invitation to give these lectures.

I would like to pay tribute also to the co-operation between the Diocese of British Columbia and the Centre for Studies in Religion and Society that has led to the sponsorship of the work of my predecessors and myself. Pastoral and academic concerns do not cohere without effort and good will, and we saw many signs of both. The Centre, of which Dr Coward is the permanent Director and Dr Hadley was the Acting Director during our visit, is a flourishing example of co-operation between academia and religious communities. The 1990s have for the most part been a dark period in Canadian universities, and the Centre's successes are a tribute to its leaders and the scholars who work in it, to the University of Victoria, and to those in the community who have given so much to bring it into being.

I am very conscious that a short work like this cannot

contain adequate justifications for everything I say in it. Nor can the notes and references do more than indicate some further places where those interested in the themes it raises can go for further reflection. I have tried to avoid too many references to works that are only obtainable in major libraries, although there have had to be some of these. The bibliography contains full details of all the works referred to in the notes.

I had originally intended to dedicate this book to my wife. But she joins me in the wish to dedicate it to our Victoria hosts.

Introduction

One of the basic duties of a philosopher is to make clear what a particular set of beliefs contains, and what its implications are. This is a key part of the self-knowledge that has been the objective of philosophy since Socrates. I try to fulfil this duty in the first and second chapters with regard to Christian ethics. In the first, I ask what distinguishes the ethics of the Christian from the ethics of a secular world that commonly sees itself as having adopted Christian principles. In the second, I ask what understanding of human nature and its defects is implied by Christian ethics. In both cases, I hold that we can find continuities as well as sharp differences between the moral attitudes and experiences of the Christian and those of the secular person.

Philosophy's task does not end with clarification. It also has to compare one set of beliefs with others, and assess their truth. So in the third and fourth chapters I try to make small contributions to two debates. In the third, I ask how the Christian view of human nature should respond to the recognition of the claims of other religions that also seek to diagnose our spiritual ills and to offer ways of life that will cure them. In the fourth chapter I enter the debate about how the Christian view of our nature ought to be affected by the recognition that human nature is a part of Nature as a whole – that it has evolved from pre-human beginnings and shows signs of that prehistory. I chose to spend the second half of the lectures, and therefore of this book, on these two huge subjects, rather than devote them to the more traditional theological arguments about human nature, sin and the work of the Spirit, because these two subjects represent relatively new challenges to Christian belief in our time. Most of the other religions have been there as long as Christianity has, some of them much longer; but it is only now that we have detailed and universally-available knowledge of what it is that they teach, and day-to-day contact, within Christian (or post-Christian) societies, with their practice. And the recognition that we are part of Nature has been made clear to us in two ways over the last one and a half centuries: by the profound impact of evolutionary biology, and by the way popular consciousness has absorbed environmental concerns. In the fourth chapter I suggest that the continuities between the religious and secular moral consciousness that I stress in the first two chapters can help us address some of the perplexities that our place in Nature gives rise to in the Christian mind.

These debates are relatively new ones, and no one addressing them can expect to do more than start discussions. But I write as a member of the Anglican Communion, and I think it is an obligation for the Christian to confront the intellectual perplexities to which Christian commitment gives rise – just as it is an obligation (though perhaps a lesser one) for the non-Christian to decide what resources Christian belief has to resolve those perplexities. Only a brief immersion in the arguments they generate can discharge these duties. That is why, even though the writer of a short book is tempted to restrict it to a few definite results, I have chosen instead to open up enormous questions.

What is the Christian Ethic?

I begin by asking what is different and distinct about Christian ethics – that is, about the way Christians arrive at their moral decisions. We who live in Western Europe and North America all know that we live in a society where Christianity, though probably still the majority religion, coexists with many other religious faiths, and where many would say they have no religious faith at all. Such a society works because its citizens have developed ways of arriving at many decisions that can be agreed upon by Christians and non-Christians alike. It also works because it has developed an attitude of tolerant acceptance on many matters where its members have differing moral opinions. But there is, of course, a third fact that helps to explain why a society that is not itself Christian nevertheless has little difficulty accommodating the moral convictions of those of its citizens who are: it is that a great many Christian moral convictions and principles have been absorbed by the secular world in which Christians live. Many who would agree they are not Christians would nevertheless say at the same time that they are adherents of Christian morality.

A Christian has to view this fact as a good thing. But it makes the question that I have put as my title a more difficult one to answer. Suppose we were to take a group of strangers, knowing only that some of them were Christians and some of them were not, but were wholly secular persons. (For the present I will take the great liberty of oversimplifying my enquiry by not including adherents of other religious traditions, as I shall be considering some of the questions that the specifically *religious* pluralism of our world raises in Chapter 3. I will note now that, with the exception of Judaism, Christianity is the major world religion that has had to contend most with the scientific secularization of the cultures where it has been dominant, although all of them increasingly will have to contend with this.) Suppose, to repeat, we were to take a group of strangers, knowing only that they were a mix of Christian and secular persons. Suppose then we were to try to discover what was distinctive about the moral stances of the Christians among them. Indeed, *was* there, or could there be, anything at all distinctive in their moral stances?

One immediate difficulty would be that we could not tell who were the Christians and who were not by observing what decisions they took on controversial moral questions like gay marriage, capital punishment, or embryo research. For these questions seem to divide the Christians as well as the non-Christians. This is true even though, once we asked them about their religious positions, some of the Christians would offer the fact that they *were* Christians as one of the reasons why they took the position they did! If we got into detailed discussions of these moral issues with them, a great deal of what they said would, *inevitably*, be the same as what was said by those among the non-Christians who reached the same decisions on those questions. This would be inevitable, partly because the moral issues that beset us at particular times are bound to be a result of the circumstances of those times, and many of these circumstances were not even imagined when the Christian church began. All of us, Christian or not, have to do the best we can in the face of the problems that confront *us*. If you are looking for what distinguishes the Christians from the others, while recognizing that it cannot only be their conclusions, you have to look at what they bring to the making of those conclusions, and to their attempts to carry them out. It is this, and its implications, that this book is about.

Before I offer an answer to this question I want to say a little more about why it is a serious difficulty. For many centuries it was a standard assumption among moral thinkers that there was some necessary connection between being a responsible moral agent and believing in God. For example, John Locke, who was the major pioneer in Western thinking about religious toleration, was not prepared to extend toleration to atheists, because he shared the popular conviction that atheists were untrustworthy persons whose commitment to moral conduct was bound to be suspect.[1] This position is no longer one that many in our society would subscribe to. There have been two sides to this change, both of them to be found both at the popular level and in moral philosophy. The first is the recognition that atheists can indeed be upright citizens and regularly are. The second is the recognition that moral judgments are, in many clear ways, quite independent of the religious commitment of those who make them.

This has to be spelled out with care, but for our present purposes I do not think I can do better than to illustrate it by reference to my favourite Anglican thinker, Joseph Butler.[2] Cardinal Newman described him as the greatest name in the Anglican Church. Butler is best known nowadays as a moral philosopher, but his moral philosophy is to be found in a famous collection of Sermons. In those sermons he propounds the view that human nature has a moral structure, and that the highest authority within that structure belongs to what he calls conscience. We tend to use this word to refer to a voice within us that chides us when we are about to do something we should not, or to evade doing something that we should; he uses it more widely to refer to our natural ability to make moral judgments, both about our own conduct and the conduct of others. If we do not do what our conscience tells us to do, or insist on doing something it tells us not to do, he says we are behaving in a way that goes against the grain of our natures. We are acting in a way that violates our own psychological structure. Now what is of particular interest for present purposes in these sermons, which are still widely used as texts for students of ethics, is that although Butler clearly thinks, as a Christian bishop, that the psychological structure he describes is given us by God, he never uses this as an argument in favour of conscience's authority. He restricts himself to arguing that if we do not recognize its authority we are doing violence to our own natures. His argument is psychological, not theological. This is partly because he wants to convince listeners who do not share his theological convictions; but it is also because he sees our power of making moral judgments as a *natural endowment*. It is like our ability to perceive objects around us through our senses: this is a power that God has given us too, but we do not need to be attending to this fact, or even to believe it *is* a fact, in order to perceive correctly. Our recognition of what is right or wrong has the same independence. He takes as the text on which he preaches his second sermon (the one in which he argues for the supremacy of conscience in human nature) Paul's statement in Romans 2.14 (AV) that 'when the Gentiles, which have not the law, do by nature the things contained in the law, these, having not the law, are a law unto themselves'. His use of this text shows that he thinks his position is scripturally as well as philosophically sound. He obviously supposes that Paul believes that the Gentiles, who do not have available the detailed set of divine commands that constitute the law, nevertheless can judge what is right or wrong in many instances as successfully as if they did.

This brings me naturally to a position that many secular philosophers regard as a philosophical commonplace, and which many of them would offer in defence of the thesis that morality does not depend in any way upon religion. It is a position that they derive from Socrates, as he is depicted in one of Plato's most widely-read dialogues, the *Euthyphro*.[3] Euthyphro is a priest, who has shocked everyone, Socrates included, by prosecuting his own father, who has been indirectly guilty of the death of a peasant on the family estate. Euthyphro regards his surprising action as religiously required because the peasant's death has brought contamination upon the family. When Socrates asks him why he is doing it he says that he is doing it because piety requires it. Socrates then asks him what piety consists of. He wants Euthyphro to give him a definition. Eventually Euthyphro obliges: piety, he says, is doing what is pleasing to the gods. Socrates then asks him whether pious behaviour is pious because the gods are pleased by it, or is it rather that the gods are pleased by it because it is pious? This odd-looking question can be transposed into a theistic idiom fairly easily: is an action right because God commands it, or does God command it because it is right? Which comes first? Socrates clearly thinks, as most philosophers think after him, that the rightness of actions comes before the fact that God requires them – otherwise, if God should have commanded the opposite of what he has commanded, that would be right, and obviously it is not.

There are many questions tied together here, but I want to concentrate on one of them only. Many secular philosophers seem to think that religious believers are all like Euthyphro: that they think morality is a matter of mechanically following some list of divine commands. Some have even used this caricature as a reason for suggesting that religious morality is infantile or immature.[4] But even if some forms of religious life do conform to this caricature, it is not hard to see that Christianity in its origins was not like this, and that the position that we find Jesus taking in the Gospels is much more like that of Socrates than that of Euthyphro. To take the easiest illustration, consider the disputes Jesus has with his critics about sabbath observance. He does not challenge the assumption that the sabbath rules were instituted by God and therefore have authority; but he makes it abundantly clear that these rules can on occasion be put aside in the face of the clear moral demands of situations in which animals have to be rescued or diseases cured. To maintain this is to give priority to the individual moral judgment, even if that judgment is normally guided by divine commands. For even if the form of your moral question is, 'What is it God's will that I should do?', this is a question that you have to use your own moral judgment to answer.

I realize, of course, that the Jewish milieu in which Jesus and his critics disputed questions like sabbath observance was not one in which ethics and religion were separated in the way in which Greek thought separated them. But I still think it is clear that Jesus, in taking the position he does in this matter, is appealing to the individual capacity to make moral judgments in the face of the application of a rule, even though the rule is agreed to be divine in its origin. This implies that he supposes this is what God would want us to do: to use our power of moral judgment (what Butler later called our conscience) to resolve a moral conflict.

I would like to offer an imaginary modern example of the same thing. Suppose a Christian physician has to decide whether or not to allow a terminally-ill patient to die when it is technically possible to resuscitate that patient. Suppose, further, that the physician believes that it is always wrong to allow patients to die in such circumstances. He or she might well say it would be contrary to the will of God to allow this. Now suppose, further, that this same physician, after experiencing a number of harrowing cases of this kind, comes instead to think that in certain circumstances such a patient should, after all, be allowed to die. How would this physician describe his, or her, change of mind? I think it is quite clear that he, or she, would *not* say, 'I used to agree with God that it is always necessary to prolong life when the means to do so are available, but I now think differently.' He or she rather would claim to have come to a different view about what the will of God is. But it is the physician's own conscience that has had to determine what it is. I am inclined to think that the modern notion of individual ethical autonomy, which was first clearly articulated in the Enlightenment, is not incompatible with Christian decision-making but is required by it.

I want to generalize this, still by reference to the preaching of Jesus in the New Testament. Jesus claims to speak for God; and his enemies deny that he has such authority. Imagine yourself there. How would you determine whose side to take? It would be clear enough what signs of authority many of Jesus' enemies would have: they would have the weight of generations of tradition and learning and temple practice behind them. What signs would there be that Jesus

7

had the right to claim to speak for God? Part of the answer would, of course, have been the healings and exorcisms that he practised; they would confirm the claims he made about the imminence of God's Kingdom. But he was not the only preacher who did wonders; and his enemies could (and did) suggest without absurdity that there were explanations of his actions in this sphere that did not imply any authority. I would suggest that an essential part of the answer must be the nature of the moral teaching that Jesus propounded: that his hearers would be inclined to accept his authority because of the moral vision that he held before them and the moral demands that he claimed God was making on them. And in accepting this, they would be using their own moral judgment: they would be judging that he spoke for God because what he said God demanded was a way of life that they would see, *for themselves*, was indeed obligatory on them.

If there is any truth in this, then there is at least one way in which morality is prior to religion: that we cannot ascribe religious authority to someone whose moral demands do not seem compelling to us, but can only ascribe it to someone whose demands do seem compelling. And this is surely part of the reason why readers of the New Testament still come to think that the person they meet there was speaking for God, and still does.

I do not mean by this that the moral vision Jesus holds out to us in the Gospels is one that we could have worked out for ourselves. But I am saying that our individual moral sense, that we use to work out many moral problems, is able to respond to a true moral vision when it sees one. If you like, revelation demands the autonomous judgment of the person who accepts (or rejects) it.

This will prompt a rejoinder. Are there not many people,

especially now, who do not agree that Jesus in the New Testament speaks for God, because they do not believe in God, yet would say that they accept his moral teachings? Yes, there are, and some of them would likely even call themselves 'Sermon on the Mount Christians'. Christianity has had such enormous impact on our Western civilization that many of its teachings have been absorbed into the secular culture. And isn't this just where we came in, when I asked what is distinctively Christian about Christian ethics, when we live in a world where on some moral matters Christian positions are thought to be obviously right by everyone, and the Christians divide as much as the non-Christians do about the others? And does not this show that the doctrinal beliefs that Christians have and that secular people reject do not make any real contribution to Christian ethics?

Let us now take a closer look and see what *is* distinctive about the Christian ethic, when it is not that following it involves you in mindless acceptance of divine authority.

II

I propose to attempt my answer to this in a rather hazardous way. I propose taking a look at what the records tell us about the original presentation of Christian ethics in the preaching of Jesus himself. This is hazardous for many reasons, one of them being that I am in no degree a New Testament scholar, and am therefore not competent to offer arguments in favour of reading these records in the way that I do. My only argument is that it seems to me self-evidently absurd to start anywhere else when your subject is Christian ethics. It would surely be mistaken to *start* with the Pastoral

Epistles, or with Thomas à Kempis, or with Pascal, rather than with Jesus, though no doubt all of these would be important to include in a full study. But if one does turn to the Gospel records of Jesus' preaching, one has to face the fact that there is much scholarly disagreement about the authenticity of those records, and about how far the original preaching of Jesus is really accessible to us. As a mere lay person in these matters, all I can do is to avoid commitment on as many scholarly controversies as possible, and indicate which option I am following in those places where I have no choice but to take sides.

I have indicated that I think human beings have been endowed with a capacity for moral judgment that is distinct from their religious beliefs in the same way that their capacity for perceptual judgments is. I have also suggested that it is this very independent moral capacity that has been at work when thousands have read the New Testament and have judged Jesus to be the ultimate religious authority because the truth of his moral pronouncements has struck home to them. In spite of this, however, I now want to say that I do not myself find it plausible to read the Gospel documents in a way that judges his authentic sayings to be confined to general or timeless moral pronouncements. The surgery that this forces us to perform on the documents seems to me too radical. It seems to me beyond reasonable doubt that Jesus' ethical pronouncements were uttered in the context that the Gospel records tell us they were uttered in: the context of the proclamation of the Kingdom of God.[5]

Picking my way through a scholarly minefield, where the mines have all been laid by others, I confine my judgments to the following. First, Jesus does not just preach moral truths; he preaches moral truths that derive their practical urgency from the imminence of the Kingdom. (This does *not* mean that what he says has no application in other contexts, only that if one neglects *this* context one will probably misunderstand what he says.) Second, the Kingdom is not a place or a dynasty, but a state of life in which God reigns. Third, it is a familiar fact that some of the texts in which the Kingdom is referred to speak of it as in the future, whereas others seem to speak of it as already present. I would think that it requires radical documentary surgery to insist that one must choose between these understandings, and that it would be a virtue in any reading of the texts that it would preserve the authenticity of more sayings than alternative readings would. Following this, I would think it necessary to suppose that Jesus proclaimed the Kingdom to be *both* in the future *and* to some extent to be present, or to be breaking in upon the world, so that the moral demands he made were demands that took account of both these supposed facts, not just one of them.

I shall try to remain agnostic about the other questions that the interpretation of the Kingdom proclamations forces one to face; I think, for example, of the question of whether the coming of the Kingdom entails the end of the temporal order, or the end of Roman rule, as Jesus saw the matter. It seems reasonably clear that however one judges these questions, the Kingdom is a state of life that already exists elsewhere (in Heaven) but not here; that our task here is to prepare for its imminent arrival, of which there are discernible signs already available.

What about the ethics? They are the ethics that meet the situation of those who wish to be fit for citizenship in God's Kingdom when it comes. It is God who will bring it, not they; but what they do now will determine whether they enter it or not. Who will enter? Here we are on familiar territory to New Testament readers, though in shockingly new territory to Jesus' original hearers. The ones who will enter are the ones singled out for blessing in the Beatitudes: not the rich but the poor; not the ritually observant but the repentant sinners; not the aggressively righteous but the meek; not the scribes, but the children. For God is a loving God who will go out of his way to seek these people, now rejected and marginalized, and invite them in, and will bypass those who have sought to protect themselves by following all the rules and avoiding risks. For those who have done that have given way to anxiety and have sought to allay it by clinging to wealth or respectability or correctness, and to give way to anxiety like this is to show you do not trust God to look after your needs. But if you do trust him, he will look after those needs, whatever the appearances; and if you are freed from anxiety by trusting him, this will enable you to be open towards those you have sought to keep at a distance before. You will therefore be open to love. This message is directed to Israel; but it is to an Israel that does not set itself apart but shines its light on the world and welcomes everyone into the Kingdom.

As we have seen, those who are fitted to enter the Kingdom will be able to set rules aside if the good demands it. But this does not mean that the conditions for entry are easy ones. On the contrary: famously, Jesus demands that we not be content with outward conformity to what morality requires, but insists that our actions should spring from the right motive. It is not enough to avoid sexual relationships with your neighbour's wife; you have to be free of the very desire for them. It is not morally good enough to rein in your hatred of your brother and not kill him; you have to be free of the hatred itself. Jesus requires his hearers to change their inner state – something that many would be inclined to say is beyond our control. The impulses we must be free from have to be replaced by something else, namely love – the desire to seek for the good of others without regard to their merits or to the benefits one might receive from them. The command to forgive injuries follows from this demand and is not really distinct from it. And as the parable of the labourers in the vineyard makes clear, one very quickly finds that if you give without regard to the merit of the recipient you quickly overstep the bounds of fairness.

These moral demands prompt some very hard questions. The first one is: Why should I change myself in this way, even if I can? For the risks are considerable. It may be all wrong of me to seek for wealth or position or protection, but these are nice things to have when you get them, and why should I give them up? The answer is that you should be like that because God is like that; he loves you and knows your needs and will meet them, even though you do not deserve that he should. Well, yes, the reply might go; but God has resources I do not have. I am vulnerable and overtaxed and underpaid and have high blood pressure. Surely I have every right to avoid the risks that the life of love would require?

The answer to that is that the anxiety this expresses is incompatible with trust in the God in whom you say you believe. If you really understood how God cared for you, you would not be anxious at all. You would become as a little child; and little children trust their parents and do not fret about pensions and stock portfolios, but concern themselves with their present relationships with those parents and with each other. If you were like this, you would not see the risks your commitment led you into as *costs*. You would cease to seek the things the Gentiles seek, such as rank and riches, and would concentrate on meeting your neighbours' needs instead. It is quite natural for the Gentiles to seek these things, because they do not know, as you say you do know, that God will take care of us.

In other words, acting from love requires a prior reassurance that the Gentiles do not have. In theological terms, love requires faith. The person who does not have faith cannot deal with the anxieties that our finitude inflicts upon us. But the person who is able to enter the Kingdom will be freed from them. And the Kingdom is at hand.

III

I think it is clear from the Gospels that the imminence of the Kingdom has two dimensions. In the first place, it is something that God, not we, will bring about: hence what we have to do is *prepare* for it. But, in the second place, it is also clear that preparing for it is a matter of living *now* as though it has arrived – not just making resolutions about what you will do when it does. This is the reason, I think, why there are texts that speak as though the Kingdom is here already: it is breaking in in those very places where men and women are prepared for it by living out its demands now. In saying this I am not saying anything that has not been obvious to readers of the New Testament for centuries; but I would like to look at this duality in the proclamation of the Kingdom in the light of what we have seen previously.

I began by emphasizing that moral philosophers have been right to insist on the autonomy of moral judgments. We do not need to believe in God to recognize our moral obligations to one another, or to try to live up to them. If this is true, it follows that when atheists read the Sermon on the Mount, with its demands to love and to forgive, they can as readily recognize that this is the morality we should all follow as those who think that Jesus, in pronouncing it, was speaking for God. For they can see, as well as believers can, that such a world would embody the highest good for everyone. But although this may be so, when Jesus proclaimed this morality he was not just offering it as morally binding. He was telling his hearers they should adopt it because the Kingdom was at hand. This meant that they should change their ways and adopt this new way because doing so would fit them to enter the Kingdom when it came. They would be fit to enter it because *they* had adopted it *beforehand*. This does not mean that the way of love and forgiveness is in some way an 'interim ethic' that only has validity before the Kingdom arrives, for when the Kingdom arrives that is the way those who belong to it will be found to act.[6] But since those who belong to it will be acting this way *before* it arrives, it is also clear that the demands of the Kingdom are not to be viewed as utopian demands. You cannot put them aside by saying that it would be all very well to walk the second mile and forgive one's enemies and share one's wealth if everybody did that, but that one has to compromise in the short run and adopt more realistic objectives in order to survive in the wicked world in which we still find ourselves. These moral demands have to be acceded to *now*. Jesus knows that it is a wicked world that we live in now, and that the Kingdom is only breaking in and has not arrived in its entirety, but he warns that if we sit and wait until it has come before we meet the moral demands it makes we court disaster. The personal question that everyone who heard him then or reads about him since has to answer is, 'Who is the realist?'

The demand for *metanoia*, or repentance, in the Gospels seems to me to be an uncompromising one. It seems to me also to be possible for a secular person, confronted with it, to see it as a sheer moral demand. It seems to me, that is, that someone who does not believe in the loving God that Jesus speaks of in the Gospels may still think that it is his or her moral *duty* always to forgive injuries, always to act like the Good Samaritan to those in need, always to behave non-violently, and the rest. If this were not so, the New Testament would have an even smaller readership in our society than it has now. And because it is so, Christians and non-Christians can often agree on what should be done about the homeless, or the plight of refugees, or the abolition of capital punishment, and other social questions.

The ethic that they try to share has some difficulties in it, to be sure. For example: Does my duty to be non-violent in the face of a robber extend to the way I should face the robber who tries to do violence to my wife or child? Is there no place for family ties when the demands of the neighbour become very stringent ones? (It is not clear to me that the popular stress among the Christian community on family values is a wholly scriptural one.) The Christians, if anything, have more problems to contend with in deciding these issues than their secular fellows do.

But although Christian ethics may well have this appeal to the non-Christian, the key point to emphasize is that they were not proclaimed by Jesus as sheer duties to be shouldered solely on the basis of conscience. They were proclaimed as the demands of the coming Kingdom. Ignoring them would lead to destruction, and fulfilling them would lead to communion with one's neighbour and with God. And this has remained true throughout the history of Christianity. Secular critics have sometimes said that the Christian ethic just adds a batch of rewards and punishments to its commands, and that this contaminates the motive of duty (replacing autonomous by heteronomous behaviour, in Kantian language). But although Christian writers have done their part in reinforcing this travesty by saying that unbelievers cannot be moral because they are not frightened of eternal punishment, it is indeed a travesty. To show this it is enough to point out that the rewards of the Kingdom only come if you seek the Kingdom, not if you seek the rewards.

IV

So being a follower of Jesus will not necessarily make one choose to do something that differs from what the secular moralist would choose to do. It is rather a matter of having one's choice determined by a recognition of what God is bringing about in the world, and by a reorientation of oneself towards the way the world will be when God's purposes in it are fulfilled. What differences do this recognition, and this reorientation, make?

The first difference, I suggest, is this. If one believes that God is changing the world so that his will is done in it, then this serves, or should serve, as an antidote to two opposed but equally dangerous attitudes. The first is despair. Each of us is weak and finite, and however well-intentioned our choices, we often fail, or at least seem to fail, to bring about what we seek to achieve. I may give to a poor neighbour out of love, because I can see his or her needs and want to help meet them; the neighbour takes my money and spends it all in the bar. I may subscribe more than I can afford to a charity for refugees, only to learn later that it all vanished into bogus administrative expenses. There is so much I cannot control. But if I believe that God's will is not going to be defeated, while I still may not see how my well-intentioned acts have helped to fulfil it, I have reason to be confident that they nevertheless somehow will. The common Christian term for this form of reassurance is the belief in Providence: both general Providence, or the direction of history towards the final realization of God's purposes, and particular Providence, the realization of the special needs of individuals who place themselves in God's hands. If one believes in Providence one can do what one should and not despair when one seems to fail in the short run.

The second, and opposed attitude, and it is one that is especially tempting to the religious as distinct from the secular mind, is fanaticism. The fanatic is someone who cannot let go but thinks that God's purposes will only be satisfied through his or her own obedience to God's demands. Such a person cannot do their best and leave the rest to God. But this is a failure of trust just as much as despair is. If one believes in Providence one will be able to resist this temptation. Just as it prevents us from giving up before we start, it helps us avoid going beyond our appointed task.

All this may sound as though the Christian ethic is undemanding; but this is not so. Recall that the citizens of the coming Kingdom are to act *now* as though the Kingdom is already here. This is bound to mean that they will not be deterred, as those who do not expect God's Kingdom may reasonably be deterred, by the practical enormity of the odds against them, by the fact that the forces of evil seem likely to win in the short run. One can expect that Christians will be likely to perform more acts of witness: acts that are, on the surface, sheer foolhardy cases of self-sacrifice that the secular moral reformer might well think it best to defer until circumstances are better. Such actions can seem a waste to the outer eye, but if the Kingdom is coming one must expect that Providence will ensure they are not a waste in the long run. The supreme example of this is, of course, the death of Jesus himself.[7]

This means that those who expect the Kingdom, and those who do not expect it but try to do their moral best in a world they do not look to God to transform, may share moral objectives, and may also quite often make the same immediate decision: to give to a charity, to vote this way rather than that, to marry or to nurse or to stand aside for another. But there is no guarantee of such agreement, since Christian ethics depends on trust in God's promise to transform the world, on putting anxiety and self-protection aside, and on avoiding despair of the outcome by leaning on Providence.

V

The demand to become like this is a very great demand indeed. There are two dimensions to its enormity. The first is the big leap involved in accepting that the New Testament proclamation is true. How am I to know that God even exists, let alone that he is poised to transform the world? This is a problem that gets worse all the time, since the proclamation is two thousand years old, almost, and the place does not look any more obviously on the edge of transformation now than it did then. The second is the demand the proclamation makes on the nature of those it addresses.

It demands that they turn towards God and his coming Kingdom and away from the obsessions that tie us to the world. It is this latter dimension that I wish to concentrate upon. The demand implies that there is a deep disorder within us to which the right response to the proclamation of the Kingdom is the answer. It implies, further, that we are somehow *able* to make that response, though it is full of warnings that the path we enter upon when we make it is a straight and narrow one. The Christian tradition has not only demanded transformation, but has claimed to be able to offer a way towards it. Just as one may ask, with reason, why one should believe that the world is God's domain, so one may ask, with reason, whether one is in fact disordered within in the way the Christian tradition says, and whether, if one is, the way it offers to deal with this inner disorder is effective and really available. (These are two questions: it could, after all, be that Christianity is right about what is wrong with us, but not able to correct it.)

It is, of course, artificial to separate these two dimensions. For myself, it is the fact that what Christianity says about human nature seems so true that makes it a serious candidate for acceptance when it proclaims the lordship of God over creation. And I shall not make any effort to avoid the cosmic questions when the argument about human nature requires that they be raised. But it is the Christian understanding of human nature that will be our main concern.

VI

Let us begin looking at the questions one must face when assessing that understanding. It is embodied, as we have seen, in a proclamation (that the Kingdom is at hand) and a demand (for inner change, or *metanoia*). I have said that the proclamation has been the historical ancestor of the Christian belief in Providence, which serves as the basis for dealing with despair about the value of one's actions and with fanaticism about the importance of one's own small contribution to the divine plan; but that the truth of the proclamation has to be asserted in the face of all the historical evidence of human wickedness and failure, and of natural evil and disaster. And if we look at the demand, parallel concerns present themselves. *Can* we respond to the trials of life with love, forgiveness and non-resistance as the citizens of the Kingdom should?

The obvious and boring answer is, 'Yes and No'. It is idle to pretend that we are so totally selfish and wicked that we are never moved spontaneously to respond to our neighbours' needs, or to forgive offences. Even though we are wicked, we will not give our children a stone when they ask for bread. Even when we are not moved to do these good things by our innate affections, we are capable, from time to time, of doing these good things because we ought to. Immanuel Kant, who famously thought that the only motive that is good without qualification is the sense of duty, was equally famously doubtful whether anybody ever acts from this motive, even though he agreed that we often do what we ought to do; he thought it possible that every time we do this, we are really doing it for some other, less lofty motive, like a desire for reputation or fear of authority. But most of his readers think he is too pessimistic about this. We do, sometimes, do things because we see that we should.[8] So our moral sense is enough, undoubtedly, for us, when faced with the demands of the Kingdom, to follow those demands some of the time. But although this is true, it does not seem to meet the case, any more than our New Year resolutions are enough to make us changed beings much past February. And this fact can breed a form of despair that parallels the cosmic despair about the value of the good things we manage to do. It is a despair not about the course of the world, but about ourselves, a despair that springs from an awareness of our own weaknesses.

The Christian tradition has been from its beginning as aware of the need to counteract this sort of despair as it has been to counteract the sense of helplessness that the apparent historical futility of one's actions generates. It has responded in two ways, both of them beginning in Jesus' words and actions and continuing in the life of the church. The first consists in the identification of what failings in our natures need to be overcome: what they are, how they have come to be, and what sort of obstacles to *metanoia* they present. The core doctrine here is, of course, the doctrine of sin. The second consists in the forms of aid that beings so afflicted can receive from God if they wish to change and enter the Kingdom. At the outset the primary form of help was the presence in history of Jesus himself. After his execution, the Christian community evolved ways in which those not granted his physical presence could nevertheless enter the Kingdom as a result of his words and deeds. These ways are reflected in the doctrines of atonement and sanctification. These doctrines constitute the Christian understanding of human nature, its diagnosis of its alleged weaknesses and the mode of cure it offers.

These doctrines have been the central themes of theology for two thousand years. But let us consider the way in which we, placed as we are at the end of the second of those two thousand years, must view these teachings. We have to face the fact that they were evolved in a community that began in an era when it was not understood that the earth moves round the sun, that human nature has evolved from an animal past, and in which Jesus and his hearers believed that the human race was beset by demons and that the primary sign of the onset of the Kingdom was the fact that he could exorcise them. I am not about to proclaim the superiority of 'the modern mind' : the modern mind has its own forms of credulity, and I am speaking from the conviction that the New Testament has a relevance to us and our condition that is as great as that of the words recorded in it had to the world of Jesus' hearers. But I also think that the vast changes in knowledge and culture since the first century make it genuinely impossible for us to accept some traditional versions of these basic Christian doctrines. Some of the difficulties in them have been debated throughout the church's history, and I want to look at one or two of these next. Others are clearer and sharper now than they could have been before. I have to be selective, and I shall concentrate, in the third and fourth chapters, on two of them. The first is the fact that the Christian understanding of our natures has competitors. I do not mean, primarily, the theories of Freud and Marx or the socio-biologists, though they are indeed offered as alternatives to the Christian view, and claim to explain it away. I have in mind the much more ancient analyses of the human condition that are embodied in the great Eastern religious traditions, which are better understood now in the West than they have ever been before. They present what is commonly called the challenge of pluralism; and although it is easy to offer hasty dismissals of that challenge, I do not think the contemporary Christian should resort to these. The second is the fact that we are becoming aware, to an extent that our ancestors were not able or required to be, of the extent to which we are a part of a wider natural order that determines our natures, and which exerts moral demands upon us. I think this awareness challenges the apparent anthropocentrism, or as some environmental thinkers would put it, the 'speciesism' of Christian ethics. I choose these two late-twentieth-century challenges because although the Christian literature is filled with attempts to deal with the problems I shall look at first, it is far too thinly provided with responses to these.

2

Human Nature and its Needs – the Christian Diagnosis

I have argued thus far that the distinctive character of Christian ethics is to be found not so much in the specific choices that Christians make, since these have often been absorbed by the secular culture, but in the inner attitudes that lead to these choices for the Christian. These are the result of a response to the demand for inner change that is made in Jesus' proclamation of the Kingdom. Beings who need to change are not as they should be. The Christian understanding of what is wrong with us, and of our capacity to meet the demand found in the Gospels have generated a set of doctrines about our nature and its possibilities. To explore these, I begin with some familiar aspects of the ordinary moral consciousness.

I

One of the concerns that all reflective people have, and religion accentuates, is concern for the inner condition of one's personality. In Joseph Butler's language again: if we think of conscience as our ability to reflect on our conduct, we can see that it also enables us to judge the quality of the motives that lead us to act. But this ability is often the source of un-welcome information! When we look within, we find all sorts of things that we wish were otherwise. Self-knowledge, they say, is always bad news. From its inception in Western culture in the work of Socrates, philosophy has sought self-knowledge, although his example has made many philo-sophers too confident that the fundamental barrier to such knowledge is intellectual confusion, and that the key to the understanding and improvement of our inner condition is always to be found in education. Religious preaching, at least in its prophetic mode, has made self-knowledge its central concern. The prophet is someone who makes us look at our-selves more honestly and recognize the need for repentance and reformation. The most striking single biblical illustration of this is Nathan confronting David with the realization of the depth of his guilt over his adultery and murder (II Samuel 12.1–14). Jesus' preaching as the Synoptics report it is obviously in this prophetic tradition, and was recognized by his hearers to be.

Self-knowledge should lead to repentance. What happens when we repent? It seems to be something like this. Hitherto we have allowed ourselves to be moved to act by desires or impulses (lust, greed, envy, dislike). It may or may not have disturbed us that these have moved us. But now it does. We recognize the power of these motives, and we acquire a desire to free ourselves from them.

There is nothing intrinsically religious about this. The con-tribution of the major religions of the world is rather to cause their adherents to do it in a more radical way. They paint a much gloomier picture of the inner condition of the human personality than secular common sense does: they emphasize the ugliness and the compulsiveness and the iron grip of bad motives to an extent that common sense will usually reject, and they dismiss as inadequate the common-sense cures and forms of self-improvement with which we all try to deal with them. So they appear to common sense to be pathologically pessimistic about our inward condition. On the other hand, they are much more optimistic than common sense is about what human beings can achieve inwardly if they recognize their failings and follow the path that religion dictates. This makes common sense dismiss the religions not only as pathologically negative in their diagnosis of the human condition, but also as naively utopian in their positive expectations.

Whoever is right about this, it is clear that we all, to some extent, recognize that if we are to come anywhere close to meeting our moral standards, we have to change inwardly as well as outwardly, since our actions are the results of the desires and impulses that we have, and it is these that make us do the things we regret. When we come to this recognition, we find ourselves in a state of inner conflict. We have desires that we wish we did not have, or had less strongly. This does not always come with a moral dimension. A simple non-moral example is that of some desire or craving that I have that is bad for my health. I may have a craving for tobacco or a drug that is damaging me physically; the realization of this leads me to want to stop yielding to this desire, and ultimately to stop *having* it.[1] My recognition of the harmfulness of this desire generates a competing desire to suppress it, or weaken it. I may still want tobacco, but I also want not to want tobacco. This is quite a complex state of mind, and it seems distinctively human. But although this state of mind is not necessarily moral, it most often does come with a moral dimension: I may well wish I did not have, or did not so often yield to, a desire that I have that results in morally bad actions. I may, for example, be prone to be irritated with all the slow drivers in front of me and lean on my horn, when all this achieves is a tenser and more dangerous traffic situation; and I may, when I get home, resolve not to yield to this peevishness any more. On the other hand, I may have a desire that I feel is too weak and ought to control more of my actions than it does. I am moved to give generously to some charities that relieve a problem that has affected me, but am not moved as strongly by others that I realize are just as deserving. Now conflicts about our motivational make-up are debilitating if they are not resolved, but some conflicts of this sort are essential for any moral development. We think of people as well-integrated, or at ease with themselves, or as having achieved what is sometimes called self-identity (having 'found themselves') when they have a clear understanding of the desires that move them and are mostly moved by the ones they want to be moved by – when they are able to identify with the desires they have. Unfortunately it is possible to identify with bad desires as well as with good ones, and we then can get a well-integrated and very wicked person. But although this is indeed a real and unfortunate possibility in human nature, I put it aside for the moment and would like to think about cases where men and women are confronted by desires that are at odds with what they think they ought to do, or refrain from doing; cases, that is, where a well-integrated person would be a good person.

It is easy to think of such cases in our own experience. To stay with purely secular examples, imagine the gambler or the drug addict or the spendthrift or the sloth, who is motivated by a wish to be more true to their family responsibilities.

Such a person is clearly in conflict, and is in a state of transition. He or she is trying to contend with a dangerous inner weakness and to distance himself, or herself, from it. Such a person has, we would say, identified with the desire to care for the family and rejected the desire to gamble or take the drug or drift. This is not to say that this rejected desire will never lead them to act any more; but if it should do so, this will be seen as a *lapse*, with which the agent will contend, or about which they will feel guilty to an extent they did not before. When someone has progressed to this position we might say that he or she has managed to treat the rogue desire as *alien*, or *external*. This language is the inverse of the psychological jargon where it is said that the moral judgment against the desire, which the agent used to hear from others, has now been 'internalized' by the agent. Instead of saying that some outside force, such as social disapproval, has been made to function within us, here we say that some force (a desire or passion) that is undoubtedly within us, has been reduced to a status where we can think of it as external to us, as somehow separate from us or alien to us.

Let us look at two examples of this phenomenon, which will help to make clear how familiar this way of thinking actually is. The first example I will take is a non-religious one. It comes from a play written in 1607 by a contemporary of Shakespeare named Thomas Heywood, called *A Woman Killed with Kindness*. A character called Sir Charles Mountford has quarrelled over a foolish wager with Sir Francis Acton, and in the quarrel he has been responsible for the deaths of two of Sir Francis's servants. Although he has come out on top of the quarrel, when his emotion subsides he recoils from what he has done:

My God! What have I done? what have I done?
My rage hath plung'd into a sea of blood,
In which my soul lies drown'd. Poor innocents,
For whom we are to answer. Well, 'tis done,
And I remain the victor. A great conquest,
When I would give this right hand, nay, this head,
To breathe in them new life whom I have slain.
Forgive me, God, 'twas in the heat of blood,
And anger quite removes me from myself;
It was not I, but rage, did this vile murder;
Yet I, and not my rage, must answer it.
Sir Francis Acton he is fled the field,
With him, all those who did partake his quarrel,
And I am left alone, with sorrow dumb,
And in my height of conquest, overcome.[2]

In spite of the fact that Sir Charles addresses God in this speech, I think we can take it as a non-religious example, because what he says to God he might well say to anyone: that although he acknowledges that *he rather than anyone else* did the murders, so that he, and no one else, has to pay any penalty for them, it was done by the passion of anger within him, which somehow took over from him. *He* is not to be identified with it, or it with him; *he* is the more peaceable being who mourns his victims' deaths, and he dissociates himself from the passion that caused him to kill them. He says this while fully understanding that he has to answer for the action that his anger has led to. So we may sum up his judgment of what has happened by saying that although he knows, and regrets, that the anger that welled up in him was indeed within him, somehow in spite of that it is external to him.

How should we evaluate this way of speaking about our own motives? One, tough-minded, way is to say that it is a self-serving piece of deception. If I act from some desire that I have, I am the one who does the action and I have no right to suggest diminished responsibility by pretending the desire is outside my real self. Most of us, however, would feel this is not merely too harsh but might well be uncomprehending in another way. Suppose, for example, that we have known Sir Charles all his life, and are aware that he has always had trouble controlling his temper; but he knows he has this problem, and has exerted great efforts to avoid returning insults, has publicly forgiven injuries, and has hitherto followed a clear policy of eliminating the power that his tendency to rage has had to influence his conduct. On this last occasion, however, he has lapsed into his former ways and he now bitterly regrets it. If we knew all this we would, I think, be more inclined to give credence to his suggestion that the anger that led to this last action was not part of his inmost self, even though it did indeed lie within his soul. We would think of him as we think about people who have given up smoking but still have occasional tobacco cravings and might even succumb occasionally; such people have managed to distance themselves from the cravings they still have, because they do not usually control them. We would, on the other hand, dismiss Sir Charles's pleas if he has been losing his temper many times a day for as long as we can recall, and has never shown any prior signs of learning from his errors. In such a case the fit of rage that led to this last action would not be a *lapse*, but a symptom of a regular pattern. This would be true even if he is remorseful every time he has given way. To have gnawings of conscience is probably necessary for externalizing a morally bad desire, but these gnawings have to be effective for this to amount to success. Without wishing to protract this further, I suggest we are willing to accept that people can have desires that they do externalize. It is sometimes right to say that a desire I have is external to me, even if I keep on having it. For I have, in some way we can articulate, rejected it.

But although this is true, it gives rise to a difficult problem. I have said so far that a desire I have can be called external to me if I try to disown it and manage to prevent it having more than an occasional power to control what I do. But people sometimes manage to tame desires in that way, and their friends and their enemies say they have made a mistake. They say they are living an unnatural life – a description that implies that the desires they are externalizing are part of their inmost natures, and *can't* be externalized. They are judged to have made a mistake about what their inmost natures are like. We can do this positively as well as negatively. I may be convinced that it is my built-in destiny to be an opera singer, whereas my friends can tell only too well that identifying myself with that desire shows a lamentable lack of self-knowledge because I am tone deaf. But to stay with the negatives, I may deliberately adopt a way of life that entails ascetic practices that others insist are beyond me. A celibate way of life, for example, is said by many to be one that denies a person's identity as a sexual being; so the monk who manages to resist all his overt sexual desires would be judged to be frustrating or denying his real nature. To take an even more topical example: we often hear it said that for generations homosexuals have been denying their real natures by trying to reject or marginalize their homo-erotic impulses. They ought instead, on this view, to 'come out', that is, acknowledge those impulses openly and not attempt to follow a way of life that tries to externalize them. This seems to be the message, for example, of E. M. Forster's novel, *Maurice*. The two male characters of this story take opposite paths in relation to the homosexual bond that has hitherto united them. Maurice ends by living a physically homosexual life, Clive by marrying and attempting to reject his previous inclinations. Forster clearly sides with Maurice. (The novel lay unpublished for almost sixty years.) The judgment here is that homosexuals who treat their sexual orientation in the way that reforming alcoholics treat their desire for alcohol is *mistaken*, whether or not the attempt to suppress the rejected inclination is successful.

Now if we think in this way we do not say merely that a desire or passion that someone has is external or internal depending on their own attitude towards it; we imply that a person's attitude towards it can be right or wrong, depending on that pereson's understanding of what his or her nature is. Once you get to this point, however, you open up a hugely complicated question: How does one tell what one's real nature is? Who do we ask to enlighten us?[3] The field, of course, is a very crowded one: we can look to psychologists, metaphysicians, geneticists, neurophysiologists – the list is very long. I want now to turn to what the Christian tradition has had to say about this matter, noting just before I do it that we now live in a world where anything it says has lots of competition.

II

The Christian tradition is, of course, very varied. On this matter I shall once again turn to a New Testament source. I begin with a quotation that all Christian readers will recognize. It is the classic place where the device of externalizing inner impulses is used.

> For we know that the law is spiritual; but I am of the flesh, sold into slavery under sin. I do not understand my own actions. For I do not do what I want, but I do the very thing I hate. Now if I do what I do not want, I agree that the law is good. But in fact it is no longer I that do it, but sin that dwells within me. For I know that nothing good dwells within me, that is, in my flesh. I can will what is right, but I cannot do it. For I do not do the good I want, but the evil that I do not want is what I do. Now if I do what I do not want, it is no longer I that do it, but sin that dwells within me.
>
> So I find it to be a law that when I want to do what is good, evil lies close at hand. For I delight in the law of God in my inmost self, but I see in my members another law at war with the law of my mind, making me captive to the law of sin that dwells in my members. Wretched man that I am! Who will rescue me from this body of death? Thanks be to God through Jesus Christ our Lord!
>
> So then, with my mind I am a slave to the law of God, but with my flesh I am a slave to the law of sin.[4]

We have moved here from Christianity's founder to its first great theologian. If we compare what Paul says with the secular thinking about unwelcome desires that we have been considering hitherto, we can see differences along with the similarities. (To bring them out, I have to include some teachings that are not explicit in the passage quoted, but appear elsewhere in his writings.) In the first place, Paul's concern seems much more *general* than that of anyone who is fighting an unwelcome craving or passion, although he is never reluctant to use those things as examples of his views. We can, after all, fight unwelcome cravings by avoiding those occasions when they are liable to surface – as alcoholics can help fight their craving by avoiding parties. That would not help the problem that Paul has. He seems to be anxious about all of his actions to which 'the law' is relevant. Now anyone who is even slightly familiar with the Jewish law to which he is referring will know that it is noteworthy for having something to say about virtually the whole of human life. And the concern that Paul has is not one that can be dealt with by saying that, as a follower of Christ he has accepted that the law can be summed up in the commands to love God and to love one's neighbour; for those two summary commandments were intended between them to be relevant to all occasions. Paul is telling us that he is in trouble every time he is in a situation when he realizes that there is something he ought to be doing or something he ought to be avoiding. On these occasions, he inwardly wants to do what he knows he ought. But something within him makes him do what he knows he should not – something that he does not, deep down, really wish to do. When he wants to do the right, only the wrong is within his reach.

To be clearer here, Paul is not saying that *all* of his desires are bad. On the contrary, he has desires for those things that the law tells him he should seek. His problem is that these desires, though they are there, and although (given the detailed pervasiveness of the law) this means there are many of them, these good desires are ineffective, and are crowded out by other, stronger, ones. Joseph Butler, much later, emphasized the distinction between the strength of a principle in our natures, and the authority it has. Conscience, he says, has authority, but not always the strength it ought to have; so although we know very well what we ought to be doing, we do not follow that knowledge but allow it to be crowded out by some form of self-indulgence. Paul tells us that this happens time and time again.

This text shows how religion, in its prophetic mode, paints a darker picture of our natures than common sense ever can. It is darker because it says that our choices are almost *always* tainted. It is not surprising that Paul ends the passage by saying he needs to be rescued. The picture he paints is one that is otherwise hopeless; there is, it seems, no chance whatever of escaping from it without outside help, help from God. To put it in the context of Jesus' preaching, we could say that it is only because God is about to bring in his Kingdom that we have a hope of changing our moral condition.

It is worth noting, though I shall not develop this because I do not know how to, that when Jesus tells his hearers that the Kingdom is at hand, he then tells them to change in preparation for it; which seems to imply that once we are inspired by the hope of its coming, we can, ourselves, turn around to fit ourselves to enter it – or at least those who are able to join him and follow him can. Jesus is unambiguous about the pervasiveness of wickedness ('If you then, who are evil, know how to give good gifts to your children, how much more will your Father in heaven give good things to those who ask him!' Matthew 7.11) and he emphasizes that the way to the Kingdom is hard ('For the gate is narrow and the road is hard that leads to life, and there are few who find it', Matthew 7.14), but his teaching seems to imply that some at least can themselves follow the way he demands. Paul seems more pessimistic, and to tell us that all our choices are tainted and we are incapable of reorienting ourselves.

This condition is, of course, sinfulness, and Paul offers a theological explanation of its power over us. He speaks of it as a law in his bodily members, a disease. One has to be careful not to jump to any simple equation of the sinful and the material here, but Paul does indeed say that sin is imprinted in our bodies. His term for the body as corrupted by sin is the flesh (*sarx*). It is almost impossible for us not to express this now by saying that for each of us sinfulness is genetic. This is his explanation of why we are locked into it. Paul interprets the story of the Fall in Genesis 3 to provide this explanation. When Adam disobeyed God's command, he introduced sinfulness into the human race. He corrupted our natures. The sign of this, Paul says (in Romans 5.13–14) is that even though between Adam and Moses there was no law, since it was Moses who was given the law by God at Sinai, nevertheless between Adam and Moses men and women died. So the mortality that is said in Genesis 3 to be Adam's penalty for disobedience is also a sign that the flesh we all inherit is corrupted. Because of Adam's sin 'the many were made sinners' (Romans 5.19), even, it seems, the ones who did not have the specific commands of the law before them. Paul has said earlier, we can recall, that even those without the law have the law in their hearts; it now appears that this is not enough to free them from sin, any more than the possession of the law frees the Jew from sin. Each of us is chronically in the position of making choices in which we end up serving impulses that run counter to what we know to be the good. We are all like Sir Charles Mountford all the time.

This prompts the question here that we asked about Sir Charles before: On what grounds can Paul tell us that there is a core in his, and in our, nature that delights in the law, and wants, however ineffectively, to do right? The answer seems to be that this is entailed by the statement in Genesis 1.26–27 that man was made in the image and likeness of God. Paul seems to teach that the disobedience of Adam defaced this image but did not erase it. The sign of defacement is twofold: the fact of death, that is, our physical corruption, and the fact that faced with the continual duty to do the good, we are unable to achieve it even though we still inwardly long to do so. Paul does seem to believe, from what he says here and elsewhere, that we only incur actual guilt from failing to act in accordance with a specific moral command. That is, he thinks we only acquire the guilt of sinning if there is a specific obligation we knowingly fail to meet or a specific prohibition that we violate. I take this to be the core meaning of his saying in Romans 5.13–14 that although sin was in the world before there was law, in the absence of law sin is not reckoned. But our predisposition to do what is wrong or to fail to do what is right is a hereditary consequence of Adam's first sin; and so is the fact that each of us dies.[5]

This, then, is Paul's diagnosis of the evil condition that he finds within himself. I have already said that it is striking that Paul finds us to be in the grip not merely of one or two besetting inclinations, but of inclinations towards all kinds of actions that are contrary to what our conscience tells us. Yet he claims that in his inmost self he wants to do what his conscience shows him to be good. If we ask what reason there is for us to believe him when he says this (when he tells us, that is, that he is in the grip of an *alien* force and is not just incorrigibly bad), his answer, thus far, is a theological one: that he is a member of a race of creatures that was created by God in his image and likeness, and, of course, the promptings of conscience are a sign of that. It is obvious, though, that this cannot be the whole story. For if he is right when he says that he continually fails to do what his conscience tells him he ought to do, then he fails any test we can think of for allowing that he has won any real internal victory over the corrupt desires that are within him. He would, of course, agree with this. In fact, the whole point of his telling us all this is that he is conscious of his own inability to win such a victory, and wants us to follow him in turning to the source of rescue that he has discovered. Without it he would be like Sir Charles would be if he repeatedly gave way to his violent rages knowing he shouldn't and bemoaning it afterwards. In his unrescued state, Paul is a *slave*, he says, to the powers of sin that control his actions. But of course, even though a slave has to do what his master orders him to do, the master cannot totally control his thoughts; and the promptings of conscience are the signs that he was intended to live in another condition.[6]

What our enslaved nature needs is freedom: the right and the ability to reject the demands of the alien master. But what can achieve this for us? Every Christian knows what Paul's answer to this question is. God has intervened in history, in the person of Jesus, to emancipate us – to redeem us in the sense in which slaves are redeemed when someone pays the price for their restoration to freedom. As I read it, Paul sees himself, and us, as incapacitated by our slavery from overcoming the evil forces within us. It might look as though someone with a vivid enough vision of the good could tame the corrupt desires within in the way in which we think it is possible for someone with will and self-knowledge to tame a recalcitrant desire for alcohol or drugs by therapy and support groups. But the obstacle to this is twofold: first, repeated failures have increased the power of the corrupt inclinations; and second, these failures have built up a record that is enough to justify despair at the burden of guilt each of us carries. (This guilt is enormously increased if one thinks that the past failures one carries are failures to fulfil one's duties towards God as well as those one has to other people. To become convinced of the reality of God is to become convinced that one's failings are immeasurably deeper than one used to think: it is to realize that they are *sins*. Atheists cannot be against sins – they cannot admit there are such things.) Think back again to Sir Charles: his ability to conquer his rages would be immensely hindered by his giving way to them time and again, of course; but his ability to go forward free of their power would be crippled if he were unable to reconcile himself to those people he had injured when he had given way to them. Even if he ceased to act violently, the power of his remorse, left to itself, would merely create a sense of worthlessness and isolation. It would not liberate the better self that he thinks lies within him, but smother it. The problem would be deeply compounded if he were to fail in attempts to be reconciled with those who survived the effects of his rages – if they were to refuse him forgiveness.

So Paul follows his grim diagnosis of our inner condition with a prescription for a cure, a cure that God has made available. Just as the core of the diagnosis is the claim that each of us is corrupted in consequence of the first sin of Adam, the core of the prescription is the claim that each of us has the opportunity to partake of the liberation offered by Christ.

When Jesus was present in the body, he could assure the sinners he encountered of the forgiveness of their sins, and could provide them with ongoing spiritual sustenance and inspiration. Paul tells us that his death and resurrection enable those of his followers who follow him in his physical absence to partake of both these sources of strength and reformation. By sacrificing himself for us, Christ atones for our sinful acts; and by sending his Spirit he provides the nourishment that enables us to lead changed and liberated lives. Together, these provide us with the chance for the *metanoia* that Jesus demanded of his hearers when he was physically present.

III

This, then, is the vision of our nature and its needs that Paul gives to us. The core of his account of our needs is the claim that each of us is in the grip of an alien power that corrupts our desires and governs our conduct in the face of our inner recognition of the good. The claim that it *is* alien is based on the divine intent at creation that we should be in harmony with God. What the death and resurrection of Christ makes possible is the restoration of this harmony and the release of the true or inner self that has been in bondage since Adam's transgression. We are offered the opportunity to be freed from the burden of guilt and the chance of sanctification by the Spirit. The vision he gives us raises many questions that are at the core of most theology. I will confine myself to two.

The first is this. Paul has some notorious difficulty in explaining the obvious fact that those who are thus freed by the Spirit still commit sins. I do not refer here so much to his wish to dismiss those who suggest that sins might now be

justified by the grace that they make possible; the perversity
of this suggestion is obvious. I think rather of the fact that he
needs to engage in moral admonitions that a superficial reading of what he says about release and regeneration might
suggest should be unnecessary. How are we to understand
what is happening when someone who is, in Paul's language,
'in Christ', still offends?

We can express this problem in terms of the way that
Christians often speak of their condition today. They often
speak of one another as being 'saved', and it is clear that
when they do they suppose that a person so described is deci-
sively different from what he or she was before. But from
outside the change is often far less noteworthy than this
would lead one to expect. If a convert has been domineering
or long-winded or obsessive in the past, conversion is likely
to produce some changes in direction, but these characteris-
tics are likely to persist in the new context: he or she is likely
to try to dominate the vestry, or preach for far too long, or
be tediously obsessed with pet causes. But this is not surprising. In so far as Paul may have been surprised by it, it would
have been only in consequence of a slowness to recognize
that the task of sanctification is a co-operative one and is
often slow. While it is in progress there are lapses. But that
is now what they are. If the old compulsions win out now
and again, they do so during a personal progress that ensures
they are externalized: that is, they are not merely due to
sources outside the core self, but are being gradually robbed
of power and frequency and are on the way to ultimate elimination. To return to Paul's own scheme, the spirit within the
regenerate person is nourished by the Spirit of God and will
ultimately be released from the pull of the flesh. Here we are
on the threshold, of course, of Paul's teaching about the

resurrection of the dead, a teaching that is clearly entailed by what he tells us about sanctification. But I cannot follow that here.

I want instead to look at a second issue that complicates the picture of Paul's anthropology that I have been drawing. We can see that the doctrine that our sinful desires are signs of our being in the service of an external power is a doctrine that has hope built into it – the hope that each of us might have the chance of being rescued from that power, of being freed. But Paul often appears to speak of the new state of the saved person as one in which he is *not* free, but rather the vehicle of a higher power, the slave of a new master.[7] The love he is able to show is not his, but God's. The fruits of his endeavours are the fruits of the Spirit. So in terms of the scheme of thought I have been using – aren't all these new features of the repentant and baptized sinner still external? Hasn't someone else (admittedly someone much better!) taken over?

Imagine a modern Sir Charles. Overwhelmed by his own shortcomings, and being politically correct, he goes to a therapist. It is clear that none of his acquaintances are going to accept him unless he changes. So the therapist, whom he has chosen because he promises quick fixes, hypnotizes him. While Sir Charles is under hypnosis, he is told that whenever other people act towards him in the future in ways that have tended to provoke his rages in the past, he will henceforth respond with sweet reasonableness and kindly gestures. Afterwards Charles is in a chronic state of post-hypnotic suggestion, but only the therapist knows this. Everyone marvels at how Sir Charles now loves everybody. Now it is clear that in a way Sir Charles has got what he has paid for; it is also clear that his fellows will breathe easier when they meet the new Sir Charles than they used to with the old one. Things are better. But Sir Charles has not really changed; for although he went into the therapist's office of his own free will, he is not otherwise responsible for the actions he performs now: we would even hesitate to call them 'actions' at all. He is a benign zombie. This is not what patients hope to get when they go to therapists, though perhaps some might settle for it. Most hope to be helped toward freedom from their compulsions, not merely to have these compulsions replaced by others, even if the others are socially more acceptable.

I think those who read Paul as saying that he himself has no role whatever in the changed life he now leads in Christ are thinking of the condition of the repentant and baptized sinner as being like that of our imaginary Sir Charles. But I do not think that the fact that repentant and baptized sinners give God the credit for their changed state is to be read this way, as though the change is one that leaves them with even less autonomy than they had before. For example, even though Paul gives us the greatest of all descriptions of what love is, one of the most influential modern accounts of Christian love, that of Anders Nygren, describes the human being who manifests it as a mere channel or vehicle of divine love. The ground he gives for this is the incorrigible self-centredness of human love (of *erōs* as opposed to *agapē*).[8] A full understanding of these matters is no doubt unavailable to us; but it does not seem to me that the language of liberation is appropriate unless at least some form of ongoing interior consent on the part of the liberated soul in the face of the promptings and infusion of the Spirit is assumed. In the language I have been using, the desires for good that are now found in the soul may have an outer source in God, but they must be there and grow and control human choices with the ongoing consent of the former sinner, and thus be internalized. Only thus can we say that the spirit within has been released so that the leftover desires of the old person are marginalized and marked for elimination. The inmost self that delighted in the law of God has been released and restored to the condition that was intended for it at creation. Even if the source of its ongoing inspiration is outside it, it is freely open to that inspiration. Even those inspired by the Spirit are themselves free agents.

IV

Paul's anthropology has been the basis for the Christian theology of the human person ever since he wrote it. There have been four main areas of discussion and dispute through the centuries. They are, of course, related; but it is possible to distinguish them, and one's position on one does not totally determine one's position on the others.

I have already touched upon the first. The sanctification of the redeemed person has sometimes been thought of as a process of solely divine activity and sometimes as a process in which the human subject has some degree of agency and responsibility, however modest. Whatever position is taken, it can be regarded as an attempt to resolve, or lessen, what is often called the 'paradox of grace':[9] the apparently inconsistent claims that the redeemed person gains in merit and performs good acts yet is able to do so solely through the active grace of God. There are also disagreements about whether the sanctification process takes place primarily through participation in the sacraments, or through the corporate life of the church community, or through inner spirituality.

These questions are connected with the issue of the relative importance of freedom from past guilt and current spiritual progress towards sanctity. Some have even held positions that appear to imply that salvation is purely a matter of God imputing innocence to former sinners, and that the soul-making process is otiose; on this view, which does not seem at all Pauline, the spiritual life is a continual round of reruns of the original process of conversion. The Orthodox, and for the most part the Catholic, traditions have always seen this view as unacceptably one-sided.

The second range of problems centre round the relationship between the ongoing sanctification of the redeemed person and the ultimate saved state to which Christians look forward. It is clear that for most the process of sanctification has only progressed modestly by the time their earthly life ends. Will it be completed by the mere fact of transition to a future state, or will it continue in that state? Do the redeemed still need to grow in spiritual strength or perform penance in the afterlife? Is the time between death and the final resurrection one in which they continue to develop or are they simply 'asleep' in that time? What about the unredeemed? Are they extinguished, or condemned, or do they have a further opportunity for change and repentance? However these questions are answered (or put aside as beyond us) it is clear that the claim that the transition to a reborn state is a decisive one can only be given full and clear sense if it is agreed that the incomplete process of sanctification will have a post-mortem completion. The belief in fulfilment in an afterlife is not a mere appendix to the Christian understanding of human nature, but is an integral part of it.[10] In Paul, this is expressed by the doctrine that the redeemed have already acquired the spiritual body (or *sōma pneumatikon*) in which they will be raised at the end.

Thirdly, some of the most bitter controversies have centred on the interpretation of the nature of the predicament of the unredeemed person. Traditionally, this predicament, or state of sin, has been traced to the transgression of our first ancestor. In the position that became orthodox, he has been supposed to have ended a period of cosmic perfection through disobedience, and to have plunged both the whole human race that descends from him, and the rest of the living creation around him, into a corrupt state requiring rescue through the Incarnation and atonement. In this orthodox tradition, physical death is explained as a consequence of this Fall from a paradisaical state, and each human individual is considered to be, from birth, so markedly inclined towards sinful acts that none of us is capable of escaping from such acts by his or her own choices. Even though there has been a consensus that our condition is one that requires divine grace for its cure in every instance, there has been continual dispute about how far our sinful condition is one in which we retain any degree of freedom or autonomy. Is repentance a genuinely free option for the person convinced of his or her own sinfulness, or is that very conviction and repentance itself to be seen as a wholly divine action? If one takes the latter option, one is almost certain to adopt some form of predestinarian understanding of the operation of grace, and be inclined to take the view that repentance as well as sanctification should be understood on the model of post-hypnotic suggestion.[11]

The fourth area of major theological debate has been over the understanding of the atonement. The church has seen the work of Christ as encompassing both the sanctifying nurture of the disciple and the prior release of the disciple from the otherwise intolerable burden of past guilt. It is this release that is the source of what Luther famously called the freedom of the Christian. How is the atonement to be understood, however? Are we to assume that without it God would require condemnation and punishment for every sinner? And *how* does the death of Christ remit that punishment?[12] Many have thought that to think in these terms is to depict God as an angry despot who needs to be appeased, and that this is impossible to square with the view that God was also present in Jesus himself. However this is to be understood, there is the further question of whether the atonement is in any way efficacious for those who do not explicitly appeal to it in their own case; are those of other faiths, or of no faith at all, beneficiaries of Christ's sacrifice, or are they not?

V

All of these questions, which I have identified as traditional ones, have generated debates that are as old as the Christian tradition itself, and it is obviously impossible for me to make any contribution whatever to most of them here. I want instead to look at two aspects of these matters that I think demand some fundamental reconsideration of the traditional debates about human nature and its needs within a Christian perspective: aspects that force themselves upon us now in a way that they could not have done before our own era. I refer, first, to the very recent recognition, in our global culture, of what claim to be alternative routes to salvation or liberation from the travails of the human condition in other religious traditions that claim the loyalty of millions – a recognition that has now, for the first time, been accompanied by genuine scholarly understanding of what these traditions actually say and do. I refer also to something that has had a somewhat longer time to force its way into the consciousness of Western Christians, through their scientific education and their ethical awareness of the environment – the understanding that human beings are biologically continuous with other species to which we have obligations and from which the evidence overwhelmingly teaches us that we have descended. Both of these demand that we look hard at the tradition Christians inherit from Jesus and Paul, and see how it can relate to our contemporary recognition of these realities.

3

The Pluralist Challenge

The Christian understanding of the human predicament and its cure has given rise to two thousand years of theological debate about the nature of the atonement and the sanctifying work of the Spirit. In the next two chapters, though mindful of the history of that internal debate, I want to look instead at two sets of challenges that confront the Christian understanding of these matters today. These are challenges that have not had to be faced in earlier periods of Christian history. The first is the pluralist challenge. The second we might call the biological challenge: it is presented by knowledge about our own ancestry and the awareness of the ethical claims of our environment and of other species. In this chapter, the pluralist challenge.

I

What exactly *is* the pluralist challenge, and why should a Christian thinker be concerned with it to the extent that so many now seem to be? I would sum it up by saying that the Christian cannot avoid recognizing the spiritual *authenticity* of at least some of the other main religious traditions of the world, and that this recognition forces us to confront some very difficult questions about religious truth. To explain this judgment, I shall proceed indirectly by offering a brief summary account of the state of current philosophical debate about our ways of knowing religious truth.

In the last three centuries Christian thought has had to confront the demands of an increasingly secular and scientific view of reason that has now become the dominant one in Western society. The explosive growth of natural science since the Renaissance, which was partly due to the separation of scientific enquiry from theological authority, has given rise to a widespread conviction that science can provide us with a model, or paradigm, of how it is rational to form one's beliefs. One should form them detachedly; one should form them on the basis of evidence alone, and one should always be prepared to abandon them if new and different evidence requires it. The whole notion of authority is, of course, quite alien to this paradigm. We do speak of individuals like Einstein as scientific authorities, but we merely mean by this that they have been very successful in applying the standards that one must follow in science, not that your beliefs or mine should be based on the fact that these individuals hold them also.

It is not hard to see why this understanding of what it is to be rational can be used to support arguments that conclude religious faith is irrational. Religious faith does not arise, usually, in the same way that scientific beliefs do. It often arises through upbringing and cultural influence; and these are influences that the detached enquirer seeks, almost by definition, to keep at a distance. It may, on the other hand, arise because people listen to preachers or prophets; and preachers and prophets notoriously prey on their hearers' guilt-feelings and anxieties. Those who have religious faith frequently appeal to authority in support of it – to the church, to the scriptures, to tradition; and they even applaud one another for maintaining their beliefs in the face of what looks like contrary evidence. It is a particularly exasperating feature of religious faith that those who have it are praised for clinging to it when everything is falling to pieces around them: a time when anyone who weighs evidence dispassionately would judge it ought to be abandoned.

Faced with this negative intellectual climate, some religious believers have responded by claiming that their beliefs can be established in ways that fit the scientific paradigm in spite of appearances. For example, they have argued that one can show by appealing to evidence that God exists, or that one can show by appealing to history that the miracle stories of the tradition are true. This sort of apologetic, which is known as natural theology, has a long history in the Catholic tradition, and has always had a comfortable home within Anglicanism. It has been revived most impressively in our own day by Richard Swinburne.[1] It does, however, have to overcome the huge intellectual barrier created by the criticisms of it we find in the writings of Hume and Kant in the eighteenth century,[2] and by the fact that the strongest evidences for God that natural theologians appealed to were those of biological adaptation, which were given an alternative explanation in the nineteenth century by Darwin.

In our own time a number of influential Christian philosophers have developed another response.[3] They have argued that the scientific paradigm of reason, though clearly right for science, is too narrow to define what rationality is in all spheres. They have argued in the following way. When I base a belief on evidence, I infer one conviction from another. I infer the existence of a God who designed the world, perhaps, from my observation of the ways in which plants and animals are able to adapt to the challenges of their environment; or I infer the presence of a burglar in my house last night from the absence of my valuables and the damage to the lock on my back door. Thinking like this is undeniably rational, and science would be nowhere without it. But thinking of this form has to start somewhere. It is impossible for *all* a rational being's convictions to be based on evidence in this manner. There must be some convictions that I have that I have arrived at directly, from experience. The convictions that I get through the use of my senses seem to most of us to be like this.

Now if we recognize this obvious truth, we face an immediate question: which sorts of convictions ought we to come by directly, and which ones ought we to acquire only by inference, or on evidence? It would be absurd to spend time looking for the burglar whom I believe to have been in my house last night if I only believe one was there because I have a hunch to that effect, even when there is nothing missing and my door lock is undamaged; unless, of course, I saw someone trying to break in, directly. But if we are told that we ought only to believe in God if we have evidence, and not otherwise, that means that our knowledge of God is always indirect, not direct, and that people who believe they have direct experience of God's presence or actions are believing irrationally. But this is a wholly dogmatic and arbitrary position. There may well be good evidence from which we can infer the reality of God, so some knowledge of God may well be indirect; but even so, there are thousands who believe that they have *direct* experience of God's presence and activity in their lives, and there is no good reason to say that they are all irrational just because their belief is not inferred from external evidence.

We do not need to look far afield from our previous explorations to find examples. Those who have followed

Paul in seeing themselves corrupted by desires that they wish to reject and have turned towards God to gain help in combating them, will see God's hand at work in the still small voice of conscience that shows them they should not yield, in the relief they experience when they believe their previous burden of guilt has been lifted, and in the major or minor victories they are able to achieve in the course of what they see as their progressive sanctification. They will see all of these experiences as direct inner encounters with God.

I think arguments of this sort, that are based on the actual religious experiences of Christians through the ages, have to be accepted, and that they represent a successful challenge to the insistence that belief in God has always to be inferred from evidence to be rational. They succeed by reaffirming the central importance of *religious experience*. But although these arguments are successful, I think their success is a limited one. For one thing, not everyone who experiences the twinges of conscience views them as the still small voice of God, and not everyone who manages to suppress an unwelcome desire sees themselves as being assisted in this by the Spirit – *even if they are*. Some people who are prompted by the Spirit may incorrectly judge that the thoughts or feelings they have had do not come from this source. Similarly, sceptics are able to produce accounts of what happens in the lives of Christians that may be false but are not fanciful: they may follow the Marxists in seeing conscience as internalized social constraint, or follow Freud in judging the need for God to be evidence of unresolved Oedipal conflict, and so forth. So although it is *rational* for Christians to take the view of their experience that they do take, it is also rational for doubters to go on doubting.

But I want to explore another aspect of this problem now.

What I want to take note of is the fact that there are other advanced religious traditions that agree with Christians that real moral reformation requires transcendent help because the source of our problems is deeper than we can see, but interpret these needs and their cure in non-Christian ways. Perhaps we can write off the secular sceptic as superficial. But we cannot do this with the alternative faiths. They meet the same standard of rationality that Christianity meets: their adherents seek, and seem to find, experiences of spiritual development, of discontent and resolution, that parallel those that are integral to the progress of the Christian soul. It seems to be a matter of cultural and geographical accident that the need to seek for spiritual regeneration from beyond the common natural order takes a Christian form for some, an Islamic form for others, and a Buddhist form for others again. This can be made to seem troubling from within each of these perspectives, and becomes more and more troubling as one comes to understand that the diagnoses of human ills and the prescriptions for those ills are inconsistent with one another.

II

I have deliberately described the nature of the pluralist challenge by using some arguments that have been developed by Christian apologists in the last two decades for a quite different purpose. These apologists have been concerned to extricate us from a particular philosophical requirement, namely the requirement that religious beliefs conform to standards of rationality that sceptical critics have used to dismiss them. I have accepted these apologetic arguments, but have suggested that they do not only serve to re-establish the rationality of Christian beliefs, but that they imply that the beliefs of Muslims, Hindus, and Buddhists are rational too. In arguing in this way I have followed a more theoretical route to a position that others have reached through practical experience of co-operation and understanding in multi-faith communities. Now it is obvious that a set of beliefs may be rational and yet be untrue. This verdict is passed upon scientific theories continually. Adherents of the world's major religious traditions can and do reach this same verdict about their rivals, and this verdict is no doubt still the commonest inter-religious judgment. But there are reasons available *within one's own tradition* for being hesitant to rush to this verdict very quickly. The Christian can at least wonder whether the God who is portrayed as the Father of all would not make ways of salvation available to the millions who have had to work out their personal destinies far from Palestine, even if he has told those of his followers who heard his message there to spread their version of it as far as they can.

How ecumenical ought we to be in these matters? This is a very difficult issue indeed, and the Christian has reason to find it harder than many others find it. In spite of the many examples of commendable inter-religious co-operation and tolerance that we find in our day, especially in larger cities, I am not much impressed by the quantity of hard thinking that this question has generated. Those who have addressed these matters, however, have started to give names to various positions that can be taken up about them, and it is perhaps helpful to list them.

One obvious way to respond is scepticism. It is a standard move among sceptical thinkers since Greek times to question our ability to reach knowledge in some sphere by cataloguing the wide variety of incompatible opinions about it that exist.[4] Morality and religion have always been the easiest examples to use. In the case of religion, it is especially easy to produce examples of incompatible teachings. Jews, Christians and Muslims all tell us that the ultimate reality in the universe is a transcendent personal God who is the creator of all else that there is, whereas the Hindu tradition that is best known in the West holds that the ultimate reality is immanent and impersonal, and that even if one worships a supreme deity such as Siva or Vishnu this deity is a mere manifestation of that deeper and ultimately non-personal reality that lies within each of us. The Buddhist traditions are notoriously atheistic, and reject the quest for a deeper meta-physical reality within, seeking release rather in the full real-ization of the fleetingness and insubstantiality of all beings, especially oneself. On the face of it, these are incompatible teachings, and the sceptic infers from this indigestible variety that one ought to turn away from all of them, either by judg-ing them all to be false, or by judging that they all involve claims to truth that are beyond our abilities to decide. Most sceptics would probably prefer the second of these positions. I think sceptical arguments are often very powerful, although I find it hard to see why sceptics have claimed to find it liberating to decide that questions of this kind are beyond our powers. It has always seemed to me that reaching this conclusion makes one a natural prey to anxiety, on the ground that if one of these positions is in fact true, the in-capacity one has acknowledged is a barrier to resolving all the greatest questions.

However, the fact that religious beliefs vary so much tells us nothing either one way or the other about the truth of any of them. To suggest that a particular perspective on the truth is bound to be faulty merely because there are others, is to imply that the truth can only be found if it is possible to find a View from Nowhere, a perspective from which one leaves behind one's culture and one's finitude; and it is not even clear that this possibility even makes sense. But as soon as one accepts that possessing the truth, if possible at all, involves possessing it from within a culture or with a perspective, it becomes impossible to dismiss all known alternatives merely because there are more than one of them. All the world's religious teachings *could* be false; but this would have to be shown one at a time. And although the variety of religious beliefs may make us doubtful about our ability to reach the truth about these cosmic matters, it does not show that we never could.

If one puts scepticism aside and begins one's reflections from within one particular religious tradition (and I shall continue to use Christianity as my example), then three possible responses to the claims to truth found in the others have so far been identified by scholars. They are exclusivism, inclusivism and pluralism. It is, of course, important to remember that what are being assessed here are religions which all teach that the world of common sense and science is not all there is; that there is another reality beyond or within that world; that unless we come to a proper realization of that reality, and a proper relationship to it, we shall remain in a profoundly unsatisfactory spiritual condition that we cannot correct with our unaided human resources; and that the tradition offers a way of restoring that relationship. All these religious traditions are, in a word, soteriological; or, to use an even uglier word, salvific.[5]

The exclusivist says that he or she represents the one true way, and that salvation is only available along that way.

Adherents of other paths, however dedicated or advanced by their own lights, are excluded from it, and their only path to it is that of conversion to the true way. In Christian terms, an exclusivist would insist that the only way to redemption is through the explicit acknowledgment of the saving work of Christ, and through membership in the community of his church.

The inclusivist says that it is at least possible that members of other traditions will achieve, or be granted, salvation, but that if they are granted it, this fact has to be understood in terms of the inclusivist's own tradition. In Christian terms, this would mean that although the Muslim or the Buddhist may be granted forgiveness and attain salvation in unity with God, this is because of Christ's redeeming work. It may be that a Muslim's dedicated and observant life is accepted by God, but if that is so it is so because Christ's sacrifice has made it possible for it to be. The Muslim thus saved would be saved through a fact that the Muslim does not personally acknowledge. The most famous version of this position is Karl Rahner's claim that the saved from other faiths are to be thought of as 'anonymous Christians'.[6] Non-Christian believers can be saved, but it is Christ who saves them.

I come finally to the pluralist. (The term 'pluralism' here is no longer being used to refer to the fact of religious diversity, as it is in the title of the chapter, but is the title of a particular interpretation of the significance of that diversity.) The pluralist tells us that in spite of their contradictions in detail, each of the major world religions is a viable route to salvation. Faced with the fact that each of them teaches something markedly different from the others about what route needs to be followed, what salvation is, and what now stands in the way of it, the pluralist is forced to say that the ultimate facts about our needs and their satisfaction are in themselves hidden from us, but are yet manifested to us in these diverse and culturally-relative ways. This raises immediate problems about how the pluralist describes his or her own religious tradition: remember we are assuming that the pluralist is indeed someone who belongs to one of them, and is not a sceptic. The pluralist cannot make any claims for his or her own tradition that imply that any of the others is not a viable route to salvation, or that any of the others is unambiguously wrong about what salvation is or about what stands in the way of it; or, if he or she does make any claims for one tradition that have any of these implications, these claims have to be qualified at some stage in the expository process so that they come out as merely provisional, or partial, or metaphorical, or mythical forms of truth. It is no surprise that pluralistically-minded Christians have selected the doctrine of the Incarnation for this sort of treatment. Pluralism cannot even be mentioned without the simultaneous mention of the name of Professor John Hick, who has given it its most persuasive and learned representation in a large number of distinguished and highly controversial writings.[7]

Exclusivism is easier to state clearly than inclusivism is. Both are immeasurably easier to state clearly than pluralism is. John Hick expresses pluralism in a manner that he derives from Kant, who distinguished between *noumena* (roughly, the entities that compose the world as they are in themselves) and *phenomena* (those entities as they are perceived and interpreted by our minds). Hick calls the ultimate reality of the universe as it is in itself the Real, and says that this reality is mediated to human beings in their various cultures as the objects of adoration or pilgrimage offered us in the different faiths of the world. Each of these faiths orients us in its own way towards the Real, so that salvation consists in a progressive change in human life from self-centredness to reality-centredness. Each of these paths is a viable route to eventual union with the Real, and none can properly claim exclusive rights in this sphere. It is clear that Hick cannot call the Real 'God', as this would imply that the Semitic religions were correct and the major Eastern traditions wrong, in judging the Real to be a personal rather than an impersonal power.

It is not hard to find logical difficulties in this position, and several Christian philosophers, who have taken up a rigidly exclusivist position, have made much of them.[8] Since they see themselves as having been emancipated from a philosophical culture hostile to religion, they have not taken kindly to being sideswiped by a religious scholar. My own visceral sympathies are with Hick; but the difficulties his form of pluralism faces are formidable ones. They are not surprising, since the Kantian distinction between noumena and phenomena has always spawned intractable puzzles. If the Real is, in itself, beyond our powers of thought and expression, then it is not at all clear that we are entitled to talk of it as singular rather than plural, or as plural rather than singular. If it is beyond our powers of thought and expression, it is right to refrain from speaking of it as God, since this would imply it is personal; but in that case, how can we refrain from saying it is impersonal as the Advaitist Hindu maintains? But then it is neither one nor more than one, and neither personal nor impersonal; which makes talk about it sound rather like the language of Buddhist sutras, which are full of multiple negations.

But my problem with Hick's pluralism does not really lie here. After all, Christians should be careful when they cast stones at others for appearing to deal in paradoxes. My problem is a psychological rather than a logical one. I am unclear how the pluralist hypothesis is supposed to coexist with actual religious practice. It is one thing to have a theory about what people who practise something are really doing, whether or not they know it. It is another to have a theory about one's own religious practice and hold that theory along with the practice itself. How whole-hearted can one be about one's own religious worship and prayer if one believes that the prayer is addressed to a being who is merely a phenomenal stand-in for a reality that cannot correctly be described in personal terms, but merely *appears* personal from within the vantage-point of our culture? It seems to me that the culture-specific features of one's own religious tradition are bound to lose their devotional urgency if this sort of *arrière-pensée* is present in the devotee's mind.

In practice, in the Christian case, Hick has argued in a way that does not seem to me to depend totally upon his neo-Kantian reading of what pluralism requires. If one judges that two traditions, Christianity and one other, say a form of Mahāyāna Buddhism, are both viable routes to salvation, and that neither can properly dictate to the other how this fact is to be understood, it already follows that any Christian doctrine that entails that only Christianity is the route to salvation must be rejected. The obvious candidate, as I have said earlier, is the doctrine of the Incarnation, according to which Jesus Christ was the Incarnate God, the second Person of the Trinity embodied in human nature. It is well known that Hick has been prominent among those who have spoken of the traditional doctrine, thus expressed, as metaphorical or mythical in character, and has expressed sympathy with the Christological studies of Donald Baillie and Geoffrey Lampe,[9] which have considered the alleged uniqueness of

Christ to consist in the degree to which his nature was responsive to the inspiration of the divine Spirit. These views (which are, in traditional language, 'Adoptionist' Christologies) see the relationship of Christ to God not as one of identity but as a special example of inspiration; in Hick's higher-level language, as an outstanding example of 'reality-centredness'. Now the obvious attraction of such Christologies for one inclined to pluralism is that they take that side in an internal Christian controversy that happens to be the least unlike the view of spiritual release that is to be found in the Eastern traditions. Pluralism about the legitimacy of various routes to salvation suggests a general principle: in any internal controversy of major importance in one's own tradition the pluralist should adopt that position that is least unlike parallel teachings in the other major faiths.

I happen to think this principle is a reasonable one, even though exclusivist objections to it are very easy to invent, and it certainly cries out for more exact formulation than I have attempted to give it here. I do not think, however, that it entails the full-blooded Kantianism that Hick espouses, though it certainly does entail a reticence to spell out too many detailed features of what ultimate reality is like. (In this connection, it is worth pointing out that if it really were the case that the ultimate noumenal Reality is totally ineffable as Hick says, this fact would suggest an utter neutrality in such internal controversies, since a flat incompatibility between the traditions would be as likely as anything else.)

III

I would like to pursue the implications of this principle, using the Christian diagnosis of the ills of human nature as our source of examples. I will repeat the principle first: in any internal controversy in your own religious tradition, adopt that position that is least unlike parallel teachings in the other major faiths. To make my purpose clear in exploring it: I want to see how far someone inclined to think of all the major world religions as legitimate routes to salvation can find similarities between their different diagnoses of our spiritual maladies, and how success or failure in this ought to modify such an enquirer's pluralist conviction. Since I have suggested that a prime difficulty for someone holding John Hick's version of pluralism is its effect on continuing participation in that person's own religion, I shall assume that our enquirer retains the intention to continue wholeheartedly in *Christian* worship and practice.

So I return now to the Christian view of human nature, as we have found it in Jesus' preaching and in St Paul. I have tried hitherto to stress likenesses between it and our secular common-sense moral thinking. Let us now see how far we can find likenesses between it and the teaching of some Eastern traditions that seem, on the surface at least, to have little in common with it.

The key feature of the Christian view of human beings is the claim that their nature is corrupted through sin, which entered the world at the outset of human history through the transgression of the first human being, and which makes us unable to resist the demands, or temptations, of unwelcome desires to more than a feeble extent. Through the sacrifice of Christ we have become enabled to turn from such inner demands, to be freed from the guilt that has crippled us, and be open to the promptings of the Spirit. The primary fruit of the work of the Spirit is a capacity for love.

The great Eastern religious traditions also tell us that each of us inherits a spiritual condition from the past. (From my reading it does not seem to me to be too much to say that this understanding of our condition was thought of as an obvious fact of nature to which the major Hindu and Buddhist traditions are varying responses, rather than as part of the potentially-controversial content of those traditions.) In a word, this alleged fact is the fact of *karma*.[10] This famous concept embodies the belief that each of us inherits the consequences of past behaviour; the past behaviour, however, is not a mere ancestor's, but *one's own*. The sense in which it is one's own may be understood strongly or weakly, but the doctrine clearly teaches that I have a far closer connection with my karmic ancestors than Christianity has ever taught that I have with Adam. I am born with an individuating assembly of predispositions (that is, with a bundle of inclinations that helps to make me *me*) and in an individuating set of physical and social circumstances (that is, with a set uniquely *mine*), and both of these are the result of the choices made by my karmic forbears, or antecedent selves. I inherit an indefinitely long, probably beginningless, past, and the doings of my karmic forbears have determined what sort of an individual I begin my life as. For the set of preferences and inclinations that my karmic forbears built up has been relocated, as it were, in that physical embryo that most appropriately embodies how it was when the body in which it was last expressed came to its end. We live in a world that has a justice-system built into its biology.

Many Westerners interpret this doctrine as fatalist, but a

moment's reflection can show that it not only is not, but cannot be. If my present mind-set and circumstances are the effects of numberless past lives and the choices made in them, it follows that the choices made in each life make a difference; and the same must therefore apply to the new life I am about to begin. I may drag a large ball and chain, but I can still walk. The spiritual task is to proceed towards salvation as far as I can during this given existence, although it is not surprising that most people are supposed to have many future existences to work through before they reach it.

The main point I wish to make about this doctrine is that it combines two things that are prominent in the Christian scheme also. The first is the insistence on a spiritually debilitating inheritance, which entails that none of us starts with a clean slate but with a set of circumstances and inner dispositions with which we have to contend and for which we carry responsibility. The second is the belief that there are also spiritual opportunities for progress within us if we are ready to pursue them by seeking those transcendent sources of power to which they give us the chance of access.

At this level of generality it is also fairly easy to find analogies for the Christian teachings about the nature of these sources of power. Both Hindu and Buddhist traditions maintain that I have within me a power that (in a sense each defines differently) transcends the individual self that I inherit and can introspect. This power may be mediated to me through the acts and teachings of a god-figure or a Boddhisattva, or more immediately through a guru or teacher or master, and I may have readier access to it through membership in a worshipping or meditating community; but it is still a power to be found within, for all it is beyond the confines of my individual introspectible self. It is a power to move towards release from the endless round of desire and suffering. The differences between these traditions emerge when one asks what this release itself consists in, but all seem to agree that it consists in the realization of the reality of what lies within, as opposed to the appearances that normally absorb us. All agree that the phenomenal or observed self, with its cravings and attachment to the physical and social world, is a sphere of self-deceiving fantasies that are mostly constituted by my karmic inheritance. The unregenerate life is devoted to the service of these cravings and fantasies. This is closely parallel to the Christian teaching that each of us is the willing victim of concupiscence, or obsessive desire, in which I try to lose myself rather than turn to God as I know I should.

Within Hinduism, the Sāṃkhya-Yoga tradition views ultimate release as the return to a pure spectator-consciousness that is totally disengaged from its environment, and is beyond pleasure and pain. (It watches the dance of nature but no longer wishes to join it.) The Advaita Vedānta tradition, on the other hand, sees ultimate release as the realization not of an individual separateness from nature, but as the realization of its lack of separateness from other selves or from the ultimate self or Brahman, which is the spiritual Power that animates the world. By contrast, the core Buddhist teaching is of the sheer ultimate unreality of the individual self, so that release comes only when one fully realizes not only the falsity of the common-sense belief in the permanence of the objects one craves, but also, and more basically, the falsity of the belief in the lasting reality of the ego or self to which one longs to grasp them. We can, then, say that the two great Hindu traditions I have mentioned teach that release is the emancipation of the true self from the desires and illusions of the phenomenal or observable self; and that the Buddhist traditions practice emancipation from the self itself.[11]

These understandings of liberation offer analogies and parallels to the Christian claim that salvation comes from turning away from self-centredness and gratification towards others and towards God. And the analogies can often be pursued quite illuminatingly into details. For example, the Buddhist doctrine that the individual self is unreal looks less unlike the Christian claim that we are all guilty of pride, when we recognize that what stands in the way of our realizing the self's unreality is the way we deceive ourselves into believing it is permanent and immortal and obstinately fuel this illusion with our every choice.

But in spelling out this last analogy I have touched upon fundamental respects in which these great traditions collide with Christian understandings of human nature, even in the very places where they say similar things. What I see as the basic difference can be best seen if we look at the Four Noble Truths of Buddhism: first, all life is *dukkha* (usually translated as 'suffering'); second, suffering comes from craving or desire (*trishnā*) third, craving comes from ignorance or error (*avidyā*); fourth, release comes through the Noble Eightfold Path of right conduct and meditation. The essence of this teaching is that the ultimate enemy is ignorance; so this and the other great Eastern traditions are traditions of enlightenment. This, of course, is why the mystic, such as Gautama or Śankara, is the central figure and why it is his teachings rather than his person that makes him the centre of the tradition. In this respect the great enlightenment religions of the Eastern world are more like the secular philosophical traditions of the West that come down to us from Socrates, than they are like the Semitic religious traditions to which Christianity belongs.

Socrates draws the student to discover truth within. He believes it is there already, waiting to be uncovered. We only need to have the muddle and confusion that we acquire from customs and traditions and intellectual laziness to be removed, and we will uncover it. We become angry and resist when the teacher forces us to confront these inner obstacles (Socrates too was executed); but once we train ourselves to clear these obstacles aside we shall be intellectually liberated and be able to recognize the good. The autonomy we all need to attain is an autonomy of the intellect. This Socratic ideal is more influential in our civilization than even Christianity has been, and it is embedded in all our traditions of liberal education, which (at least nominally) centre on the release and nurture of the self-sufficient critical intellect. And Socrates is quite clear about it: if we pursue what is not good, it can only be because we do not yet understand that it is not good; for no one would be so foolish as to pursue what they knew to be bad.

But this has only to be stated to be recognized as false. Of course it is *stupid* to pursue what one knows to be bad; that one does it requires some special explanation; but we all do it, all the time. This is where we came in. Paul is telling us just this when he tells us that he continually fails to do what he knows he should. He is explicitly rejecting the Socratic understanding of the cause of evil conduct.

It is here, I think, that we find not only one of the reasons for the chronic uneasiness between philosophy and faith in our culture, but also a reason for being deeply uneasy about assimilating the Christian (and Jewish and Islamic) traditions to the enlightenment faiths.

There is another respect in which a deep contrast stands out. The process of enlightenment consists of a progressive distancing of oneself, a progressive detachment from, the world of organic life and desire. One performs one's duties detachedly, with a view to releasing the soul from the attachments that beset it and tie it down. Desire, *as such*, becomes the enemy. But in the Christian tradition it is not desire as such that is the enemy, only self-centred and evil desire; the right desire, the longing for God and the longing for the good of the beloved, are what need to be released, and their release is the fruit of the work of the Spirit.[12]

IV

I have been suggesting that there are very deep differences between the Christian understandings of human nature and its needs and those of some of the major Eastern religious traditions. I am inclined to think that the increasing influence of those traditions in the West is partly due to the fact that they diagnose our spiritual problems in a way that resembles the Socratic tradition that has dominated our secular culture since Greek times, and combine this diagnosis with long-standing traditions of spirituality that compensate for the over-intellectualism that is the main failing of Socratic thinking. Whether this is true or not, I have been attempting to point out a major obstacle in the way of the position known as pluralism.

Pluralism seems much more tolerant than exclusivism, which is clear but uncharitable, and more enlightened than inclusivism, which tries to be charitable but seems to manage only to be patronizing. The desire to avoid these pitfalls is commendable, and indeed thoroughly Christian. I share it and would like to yield to it. But it is hard to do so, and I will now add some considerations that I think make it even harder.

Pluralism, again, is the view that the major religious traditions of the world are equally viable paths towards salvation. What exactly does this *mean*? What is it that each of these traditions is being said to be a viable path towards? 'Salvation' is a term that has its natural home in Christian, and perhaps Jewish and Islamic contexts. Let us look at it in those contexts first. It seems to combine two notions: that of the present condition of the soul or personality of the 'saved' person; and that of the long-term destiny of that person. To say someone is saved is to tell us something about how that person's soul has been changed and where that person is going. I have argued earlier that these cannot be separated, since the present change is thought to be a decisive but incomplete one, and this only makes clear sense if we suppose that person is destined for further sanctification and spiritual development. In spite of this fact, there is an ongoing temptation for philosophers and theologians to overlook the future dimension of salvation and to concentrate on the observable present transformation of the person: that is, to think of salvation as *consisting in* joy, serenity, openness to love and freedom from guilt. In our century there have been many attempts to develop desupernaturalized forms of Christianity that concentrated entirely on these features of the saved state and ignored its eschatological dimension.

If we turn to the major Eastern traditions, we find a parallel duality in their descriptions of the state of the transformed person. The common term here is not 'salvation' but 'liberation' (*moksha*). The use of a different term need not be of great significance if we have reason to think we are dealing with more or less the same concept. It is not uncommon to find writers of a pluralist bent using the combined term salvation/liberation. So pluralism, then, is the view that all the world's major religious traditions are equally viable paths towards salvation/liberation. This amounts to saying that the transformed person in every tradition is following a path that will lead to freedom from the shackles that bind every unregenerate person and towards a destiny that releases the true being within. This is the best I can do to articulate the pluralist position.

But if we examine what liberation and salvation are believed to consist of, we find enormous differences. They are less enormous if one confines oneself to the present state of the liberated or saved person. They are there even here: I do not see the compatibility between *agapē* and detachment, for example; and the priority of spirituality over social commitment in the enlightenment faiths seems to reverse that found in the Christian life. But there are similarities also: serenity, lessening of self-absorption, and a capacity to live in, but not of, the world and to cast off anxiety. If these are the only comparisons to be made, then there is a reasonable degree of plausibility in claiming that the traditions that yield these results at the psychological level are equally viable paths to salvation or liberation, since salvation and liberation have these psychological likenesses. But if we turn to the views of long-term destiny that are held in the Eastern traditions, the suggestion that we can find parallel analogies is very strained. For the Christian, salvation consists ultimately in union with God in a mode of being that fulfils the individual's needs and is characterized by love of God and of one's fellows. For the great Eastern traditions, the expectation is envisaged as a state of being that transcends individuality, personality and attachment. I would submit that there is no common conception here of which any single or double term can be the name. This would remain true even if the present psychological condition of the saved or liberated were more similar than it in fact is. One cannot hold that all these traditions are equally viable paths to the same objective, for there is no common objective to which they all can be said to lead.[13]

I think many Christians see this, yet are deeply unhappy about it. They are unhappy about it because they recognize in other spiritual traditions sources of personal transformation that they honour and respect and which are as humbling and demanding as their own – and supported, often, by sharper thinking. But, if I am right, the pluralist assessment of this situation is not a fully coherent one. There is nowhere to go but to a purged inclusivism. It has to be purged not merely of patronage, but also of self-assurance. Christians may reasonably say that they know all that they need to know to be saved. But they cannot say that only what they know *can* save.

I said much earlier that the Christian view of the world and the secular humanist view that has spread so much since the Renaissance are both rational positions. Yet only one of them, at most, can be true. The pluralist challenge has arisen in our time because we can see, as we have not been able to before, that other religious traditions that base their claims on spiritual experience can make rational claims to our allegiance as Christianity can, and that it seems to be a matter of contingent circumstance which one, if any, is a live option for each of us. John Hick has said that the world is 'religiously ambiguous', by which he means that it can rationally be viewed as self-contained and uncreated and inexplicable as the naturalists and humanists judge it to be, or as created and sustained by a transcendent God as the great Semitic religions teach us that it is. The spiritual claims of the great Eastern faiths, whose power Hick has done so much to make clear to his fellow-Christians, show us that the ambiguity is a multiple one: that it is not only rational to be either a Christian or a humanist, but also to be a Muslim or a Buddhist or Hindu or a Sikh. Faced with this truly shocking embarrassment of choices, what is the honest and puzzled enquirer to do? And what is the Christian to do?

I think both, if they have the wit and the time, have also the duty to do what they can to reduce, or even ideally to eliminate, the ambiguity that confronts us – to try to *disambiguate* their world. I have said this elsewhere; and I have also said what it is a little embarrassing to say here and now, that such disambiguation is a task for philosophy.[14] It involves comparing traditions with each other, and evaluating each of them in the light of the common fund of scientific knowledge that we all have available to us and which none of us has any right to ignore. I propose to spend the next chapter doing the second of these for the Christian understanding of human nature.

4

Humans and the Natural World

In this chapter I look at the challenge the Christian understanding of human nature and its needs faces, not from secular ethics or from the insights of other religious traditions,
but from another source: from our increasing scientific and
moral awareness of the intimate relationship we have with
the world of non-human creatures. I must say at the outset
that I find the issues I have to raise here the hardest of all to
deal with in the context of a Christian world-view. To some
they will not seem as urgent in practice as the others, but that
is a view I do not share.

I

I have mentioned scientific and moral awareness. I will take
the scientific first. It is as well established scientifically as
anything is, that the immense variety of species in the world
have evolved over millions of years, and that the human
species is one example of this evolutionary process. To say
this is not to deny that there are many deep mysteries in the
process, among them two that have a direct bearing on our
understanding of ourselves: the origin of life itself, and the
origin and function of consciousness. Some of these mysteries may turn out not to have scientific answers. But it is only

in the darkest intellectual backwoods that it is still denied that the present variety of species is the result of millions of years of evolution and that the human species is also.

Some Christians think that the whole history of dispute about the compatibility of Christianity and evolutionary science is an obvious mistake; for there is no reason to think that the Genesis creation story should be read literally and the world be supposed to have come into being in six twenty-four-hour days. It would be splendid if this were all there were to it, but of course it is not. Opposition to the theory of evolution has not been based on anything as simple-minded as this: it has been the result of an awareness, however inexplicit, that recognizing its truth would force us to confront problems of great complexity. The same was true in the days when church authorities fought against Galileo. They were not only concerned about how Joshua could have told the sun to stand still if it were the earth that was moving and not the sun, though they discussed this. They were able to see that once they conceded that Galileo was not just propounding a hypothesis that enabled astronomers to predict the movements of celestial bodies, but had discovered how things really were disposed in space, many key Christian teachings would have to be interpreted to fit.[1] We no longer feel disturbed by the adjustments that heliocentric astronomy has forced on us (so that everyone could laugh it off when Yuri Gagarin said he had not run across God when he was in orbit in space). But Darwin still makes us uncomfortable, or should.

Why should he? There are many reasons, but I shall start with the most obvious, and wish to emphasize its difficulty. It is a difficulty *for Christians*; and some of them would still say, though I would not because I cannot, that it is hard enough to cause them to reject the theory of evolution.

The Christian diagnosis of the ills of the human condition is a doctrine of great power. Power in practice, because the acceptance of it by thousands has been a source of personal transformation. And power in theory, because it has led to the recognition of so many mysterious secrets in the human soul. One of the thinkers who did the most to explain its power was Blaise Pascal, who lived in the seventeenth century, right at the time when the spiritual implications of the helio-centric theory were being absorbed. He was struck by the impact of the immensities of space on human minds that had hitherto believed themselves to live in a small three-storey universe; and he is the source of some of the most moving expressions of the recognition that what gives the human being dignity and importance cannot be size or physical power but must be consciousness, intellect and spirit.

He tries to persuade his worldly and sceptical readers to turn to God, not by proving God's existence or the authority of the scriptures after the manner of earlier apologists, but by describing the spiritual plight of the human person. He does this with a power and insight that are unparalleled. What he stresses as he looks at the pyschology of humankind is the paradoxical combination of greatness and wretchedness, of weakness and strength, of intellectual might and foolish self-deception. No one has ever described it better. He describes all this without leaning on the theological truths that he wants us to end up believing. He wants to show us the deep wretchedness and the potential grandeur that coexist in each of us. He then wants to make us see that only the strange Christian story of human fallenness and the need for redemption can make sense of this paradoxical combination. He says of man: 'All these examples of wretchedness prove his greatness. It is the wretchedness of a great lord, the wretchedness of a dispossessed king.'[2] Here we see Pascal telling us how Paul's account of the Fall and the need for rescue makes sense of the inner conflict that each of us can attest to, in a way that nothing else can.

Unfortunately, however, we can no longer accept the story as Paul (and Pascal following him) present it. Not since Darwin. Darwin has not shown us that our predicament is any less serious than Paul and Pascal said it is. But he has prevented us from making sense of it in quite the way they did. We may still need rescue. But we are not dispossessed kings. We are a bunch of biological Johnny-come-latelys. What the evolutionary understanding of our origins makes clear is that the traditional doctrine of the Fall must go.

Before I go any further at all, we must ask what 'the traditional doctrine of the Fall' is. I take it to be the view, traceable to Paul, and based upon his interpretation of the story of Adam's disobedience in Genesis 3, that because of that disobedience, death and evil came into a world that was hitherto free of both, and that the deep influence of sin in the soul of each person is a consequence of that disobedience also. I take it to be obvious that if the evolutionary view of human origins is true, some parts of this doctrine have to be abandoned. Since human beings came into the world so late in the evolutionary process, it is not possible to think that the deaths and the sufferings that preceded human beings were the consequences of human choices. Mortality preceded humanity, and was not introduced by humanity. Nor can we suppose that pain, suffering or competition for resources were introduced by humanity, though no doubt they have all been augmented by human doings.[3]

I would like to quote here from *The Montreal Declaration of Anglican Essentials*, a doctrinal statement published in

1994 by a group of traditional Anglican clergy and laity. On the first page, under the heading 'Creator, Redeemer and Sanctifier', the authors of this document state:

> The almighty triune God created a universe that was in every way good until creaturely rebellion disrupted it. Sin having intruded, God in love proposed to restore cosmic order through the calling of the covenant people Israel, the coming of Jesus Christ to redeem, the outpouring of the Holy Spirit to sanctify, the building up of the church for worship and witness, and the coming again of Christ in glory to make all things new. Works of miraculous power mark the unfolding of God's plan throughout history.[4]

If we take the fact of our evolutionary origin seriously, the first sentence demands reflection. It is notable that it says that what disrupted the good order of creation was 'creaturely rebellion' rather than 'human rebellion'. If 'human rebellion' is what is meant, then the sentence implies one of two things: either all the apparent evils of the natural order are due to the rebellion of human beings (whether or not this rebellion took place as the story in Genesis 3 describes), or they are not evils at all. The former is manifestly untrue, and the latter is difficult to argue, though I shall return to it. It is possible, however, that the phrase 'creaturely rebellion' has been used in order to accommodate a possibility that has been offered as an explanation of natural evils from time to time in Christian history: that those evils that are not due to human choices are due to the interference of other free rational agents. Just as God created human beings with the freedom to do things that he did not wish them to do, so he created other agents with a similar freedom. Since freedom is meaningless without a degree of power, the suffering and destruction that seems to have occurred in the natural world before human beings existed should be ascribed not to God, but to the interference in Nature of these other agents. This view has a slight scriptural base, in two ways. It is clear that the stories of many of Jesus' healings that we have in the Gospels presuppose that many human beings are afflicted by the activities of evil spirits; their healing takes place when Jesus exorcises those spirits. (On one famous occasion he permits the spirits to leave the afflicted man and take possession of a herd of pigs that are then driven by the spirits over a cliff.[5]) The other scriptural source that could be appealed to in support of this view is the story in the book of Revelation of the war in heaven where Satan and his angels were driven out. 'The great dragon was thrown down, that ancient serpent, who is called the Devil or Satan, the deceiver of the whole world – he was thrown down to the earth, and his angels were thrown down with him.'[6] In the best-known presentation of this tradition in Milton's *Paradise Lost*, Satan seeks revenge by corrupting the first man and woman, and the other evils in the world emerge as a consequence of their act of disobedience, which 'brought death into the world and all our woe'. But it is possible to hold that those apparent evils in our world, such as death and animal pain, that cannot be ascribed to any human choice because they preceded the existence of humans, can be ascribed to independent acts of interference on the part of Satan or other fallen spirits. I shall call this the Fallen Angels theory.

Many people are inclined to scoff at the Fallen Angels theory, whether it has a base in some scriptural texts or not, and will say that it belongs to a pre-scientific era and is to the modern mind self-evidently absurd. Now although I find myself, as an inheritor of the post-Renaissance scientific world-view, inclined to react in just this way, I do not think that it is wise to leave matters there. For one thing, what is self-evidently absurd to one generation is not absurd at all to another, and the modern mind has its own repertoire of credulities. For another, it is not impossible, as far as I can see, that if there are spiritual agents at all (and remember that if one believes in God one believes there is one spiritual agent), phenomena that we now think we can explain scientifically may *also* be spheres of activity for such agents, without ceasing to be within the purview of science. We have to be clear, though, that if we say this we are not free to think of the actvity of the Fallen Angels as mere occasional interference, as a matter of their performing evil miracles, as it were. At least, we cannot think this way if we wish to blame them for earthquakes or animal pain or population fluctuations. For these appear to have been integral parts of the very mechanism of evolution. The old Fall story had Satan tempting Adam and Eve and the natural world then falling along with them, thus destroying the paradisaical character of humankind's environment. But if the Fallen Angels theory is to account for the apparent evils that preceded all human life, the angels have to be given a more foundational role than this. To explain earthquakes and tornadoes and and species extinctions they need to have had a say in the constitution of those forces that determine catastrophes in these spheres: in the structure of seismic upheavals and low-pressure systems and global warming and cooling. They cannot be occasional intruders into God's world, but collaborators in its very creative processes. This is uncomfortably close to Manicheanism.[7]

I have not proved the Fallen Angels theory to be impossible.

I will say merely that its only advantage is a dubious theological one, and that adopting it will lead to potentially heretical results.

So if we reject the belief in a historical Fall, it would not seem that we can maintain, with *The Montreal Declaration*, that the universe was in every way good until creaturely rebellion disrupted it. Unless, of course, we are prepared to say that the natural world into which humanity came was indeed 'in every way good' just the way it was when we arrived, even though it was not like the paradise of traditional stories. I will return to this suggestion later. But I must turn first to some of the moral dimensions of our closeness to other species in the natural world, and of our obligations to the natural world.

II

While it is true that the sense of closeness to the non-human realm has been brought about in part by the absorption of the theory of biological evolution, it has also had important moral sources in the environmental movements that have been so active in recent times. These movements have had more impact on some people than upon others, of course, but they are now very much part of our mainstream ethical and political culture, so that it is politically incorrect to disregard them, even though they commonly lose out to economic imperatives. There are two obvious features of popular moral thinking that we should acknowledge at the start. There is, first, a concern for minimizing the bad effects of industrial and economic development on the physical and biological environment in which it takes place. This is not only a matter of anxiety about the damage toxic wastes, for example, can do to the lakes and rivers from which we get our water, which certainly derives for the most part from a concern not to harm the human beings who depend on these resources; it has commonly expanded to include a concern to reduce the destruction of animal habitat and the poisoning of marine life. This latter sensitivity to the effects our own supposed betterment might have on the needs of other species is very widespread, and although, once again, it is not clear how much day-to-day difference this sensitivity makes to our decisions, especially when they affect our pocket-books or our vacations or our diet, it has led to a second form of environmental concern, namely a conviction that most of us would now acknowledge, that we have moral obligations not only to other human persons, but also to the members of other species with whom we share the planet. This conviction is at its strongest when we consider the needs of higher mammals, such as chimpanzees and whales, but it extends more widely to include animals that a generation or two ago we would not have thought deserved serious ethical consideration, such as chickens and rabbits; cosmetics are now marketed on the grounds, effective for significant numbers of purchasers, that they have not been tested on animals, and there is a real enough market for free-range eggs and chickens as distinct from those raised in battery farms. The pressure to increase legal penalties for cruelty to animals is strong. It is not just animals either; we are not all tree-huggers, but most of us cringe at the sight of a 'clear-cut' forest, even though we still waste paper with abandon.

This moral change, which I for one regard as a great advance, is not one for which the Christian community can take a great deal of the credit. I do not mean by this to join those who blame the so-called Judaeo-Christian tradition for the fact that our civilization has not paid heed to these considerations before. I think that blindness to what now seem to us the moral claims of other species has been characteristic of Christians and non-Christians alike, and I cannot see much, for example, in the moral thought of the Enlightenment to inspire us to greater environmental sensitivity. It does seem to me, however, that especially at the popular level, sensitivity to these matters has been the result of pressures coming from activists who are for the most part secular people, even though their ways of life may often manifest a non-Christian sort of religiousness. In spite of this, there are signs that the Christian churches are, in the popular phrase, 'taking it on board'. Indeed, they should. For rejection of cruelty to animals, respect for wild things, expansion of the moral imagination, are all natural extensions of the Christian emphasis on love and compassion and the needs of the other.[8]

For an analogy, we can look at another classic example of moral change in the history of our civilization: the rejection of slavery. The writers of the New Testament clearly all suppose that their world would continue to include this terrible institution; why indeed would they not? None of them moves from saying that their new life should change the relation between masters and slaves to suggesting that slavery should not exist. But most of us would now assume that the master–slave relationship is inconsistent in itself with Christian values. This particular realization, however logical and obvious it may seem to us in retrospect, took time to reach full understanding. The same is true for our recognition of the moral needs of non-human creatures. While the initial proclamation of the change the Christian life requires is a proclamation about our relationship to God and to one another, and although we are of more value to God than the sparrows, the fact that God knows when each one of them falls should teach us that we should consider our duties to them as well as to our human neighbours. So it is only to be expected that there has been, to some extent, what we might call a greening of Christianity; and I think in fact that accommodating this change presents fewer theological perplexities than accommodating some feminist criticisms of the Christian tradition.

I hope that what I have said so far about our current attitudes towards other species is uncontroversial. If so, then I think it is fair to describe the changes in our moral attitudes in the following way. I think these changes represent a significant evolution from what John Passmore has called a *conservationist* attitude towards nature, in which the primary emphasis is on the saving of natural resources for future human use (so that the beneficiaries of our moral concern are future generations of human beings), to what he calls a *preservationist* attitude towards nature. Passmore defines 'preservation' as follows:

> By 'preservation' I mean the attempt to maintain in their present condition such areas of the earth's surface as do not yet bear the obvious marks of man's handiwork and to protect from the risk of extinction those species of living beings which man has not yet destroyed.[9]

So to say someone has a preservationist attitude towards Nature is to say that he or she believes, strongly or weakly, that we have some degree of obligation to maintain in their present condition those areas of the earth's surface that do not yet bear the obvious marks of human handiwork and to protect from extinction those species of living beings which humanity has not yet destroyed. Many of us would admit to some degree of preservationism in our attitudes to Nature. The preservationist attitude wins out when we insist that limits are placed on the development of recreational areas like golf courses when their development would destroy wilderness, and when we in Canada insist that our National Parks be left as far as possible in a pristine state. It wins out when some dedicated naturalists succeed in reintroducing species to the wild that have been brought to the verge of extinction. And I think preservationism manifests itself in other ways also. It emerges in a common form of thinking that supposes it better, where possible, to maintain what we might call a 'natural' way of doing things even in areas where human dominance is long established. Two examples of this come to mind. There is a widespread anxiety that the development of genetically-modified crops, while producing greater food yield, will also destroy or reduce biodiversity, which is commonly regarded as in itself good, whether or not human beings benefit from it economically. And the resistance to battery-farming is based on a negative judgment of practices that prevent the birds and beasts who are subjected to it from exercising their instinctive repertoire, like digging or stretching their wings. The supermarket where we shop has a produce section where organically grown vegetables are displayed, because some shoppers prefer vegetables that are grown in supposedly more natural ways. Here some people are attempting to preserve some aspects of what Nature would enjoin if left to itself in situations wholly dominated by human choices. In other words, they are trying to have human choices follow what one would find in Nature if we were not part of it. The natural order is, to a degree, being seen as the source of a standard which we have some obligation to follow.

The increase in preservationist thinking has been given another name. It has been called a shift from the Shallow Ecology Movement to the Deep Ecology Movement.[10] These titles were invented by the Norwegian philosopher Arne Naess. They are obviously evaluatively-loaded titles, and I do not suggest that a Christian can or should be comfortable with all the evaluations associated with Naess's clear preference for Deep Ecology. But I do think that the Christian should be at ease with some degree of approach to what Naess calls the 'biospherical egalitarianism' of this movement. Christians should see their way to being at least mild preservationists.

III

What has this to do, however, with the Christian understanding of human nature? A great deal.

I have already argued that the traditional doctrine of the Fall, in spite of its power to explain those features of unregenerate human nature from which the Christian proclamation requires us to turn away, is not available to us. We have to see ourselves as beings who have descended, or if it seems better so to describe it, who have *as*cended, from an animal past. To acknowledge the special calling that human beings have must not involve us in denying that we are biological fellows of the other species whose interests and needs we are at last beginning to acknowledge as proper objects of our moral concern. It follows from this that if we are not fallen, in the traditional sense, then neither are they. We need to be freed from the legacy of the conviction that animal nature bears the marks of human disobedience and sinfulness, even when it is undisturbed by human interference. Perhaps non-human nature is the way God intended it to be, and it is self-important of us to suppose that aspects of it of which we disapprove are consequences of some choice that the earliest humans are supposed to have made. Perhaps the Deep Ecology Movement, in encouraging us to treat it with respect rather than as a repository of resources, is serving the gospel?

Certainly it can help us get away from the sorts of judgments that one finds all too often in Christian writers who try to make sense of the pain and destruction that is clearly so common in the natural world. C. S. Lewis suggested, in *The Problem of Pain*, that the proper and intended state of the animal kingdom is represented by tame animals not wild ones.[11] And Eric Mascall, an often perceptive and scientifically-informed theologian, has gone as far as to say that 'a cabbage or a sheep achieves its highest privilege in becoming the food of a Christian man'.[12] Such judgments, both, I am sorry to say, from Anglicans, hardly express the right priorities to help us determine our proper attitude to our fellow-creatures.

I shall return shortly to the issue that Lewis was addressing, namely the problem of animal suffering. For the present, however, I shall concentrate on the Christian view of human nature. So far all I have suggested is that it is proper to see some of the attitudes of the preservationist as attitudes that fit well into the Christian ethic of love and compassion. Just as one should not only love those who love you in return (even the Gentiles do that), one should not confine one's love and compassion to those beings who are even *capable* of

88

these – though of course some animals appear to be. In this respect the Christian ethic rightly demands from us attitudes that other species cannot have demanded of them.

But how are we to regard the state of unregenerate human nature? Knowing what we do of our animal ancestry, we have to judge it as consisting of many inherited traits, including many that redeemed human nature would be without, but which have served in the evolutionary process to allow human beings to develop and survive. It will also include some inherited capacities that redeemed human nature would manifest in greater measure. The former group would include aggression and dominance, the latter affection and grief. The fact that these are to be found within us is to be explained by our biological ancestry. In terms of what we would like to become, this ancestry is a mixed one. In terms of the demands of natural selection, its mixed character is readily understood.

The Christian tradition sees human beings as called to a mode of life for which their biological provenance is not a sufficient preparation; a mode of life that transcends anything that the rough-and-tumble of natural selection can make possible. In Christian terms, the biological human being is not yet fully and completely human. The classic expression of this vision of possible humanity is the doctrine that we were made in the image of God himself. Once we recognize the biological source of humanity, we have to see this doctrine not as a statement of what human beings originally were, but as a statement of what human beings have the capacity to be. To have this capacity they need the power of moral discrimination: the power to know their own natures, to choose good over evil in what they find within them, and to reach out towards the transcendent source of help that they need to enforce that choice. To have this capacity, they require a higher intelligence than the beasts, and they require freedom. The doctrine of the *imago dei* is a declaration that human beings, though finite, are also free beings who are not just biologically programmed but have the capacity to choose what is good, and of course (unfortunately) what is evil.

The Pauline picture of the human person as wanting to do what is good but succumbing to what is evil is accurate self-analysis for all of us. But we have seen reason not to accept Paul's account of how it has come about that we are all like this. Can we give an alternative account of this that is consistent with what we now know of human origins and also with the radical character of the evil that Paul has diagnosed? Many pictures of human nature that involve rejection of the Fall story fail to acknowledge the gravity of the evil within us. The ingredients that we can trace to our biological origins are, once more, our inherited impulses, good and evil alike, our superior intelligence and our freedom. These give us our capacity for moral discrimination, and what goes with this and stands at the heart of the Fall story, our capacity for *temptation*. Temptation arises when some objective presents itself as attainable, and we want it but know very well that we should not seek it, or when some objective presents itself as attainable, and we know very well it is good but find it conflicts with some other impulse like the desire for popularity or the desire for rest. Only beings that can be tempted, that have the moral wherewithal to overcome temptation or to yield to it, can sin. In *this* sense the Fall story must be historically accurate: that sinfulness could only invade our natures when we had become advanced enough to know good and evil.

But what of the mystery of the dominance of evil? To say, as the Fall story does, that it came about because our ancestors chose evil rather than good, because they yielded to temptation, would not be so very illuminating, even if it were true. It only appears so because it is alleged to have happened so long ago! Our attempt to replace this story has left out one ingredient that is addressed in Jesus' preaching, is dealt with in many Psalms and prayers, and is clearly a central element in human life, and, as far as we know, in human life alone. That is, anxiety.[13] The human capacity to understand disease, to assess dangers, to know one's own mortality, is a mixed blessing. Animals face disease, fear danger and die too, but the human recognition of the nature of the realities that beset us in our finitude makes the menace of these things far greater for us. For one thing, we are able to anticipate them all, to expect one or all of them to beset us at any time, not merely to respond to them instinctively when they actually come. What Jesus told us to do in the face of this anticipation is to trust God. But this involves a degree of reduction in our reliance on those myriad devices we use to protect ourselves: our money, our rank, our family. It also involves giving up those devices we use to conceal dangerous realities from ourselves: our forms of illusory self-sufficiency and our perverse determination to lose ourselves in play and pleasure. The radical evil in our natures comes from our seeking all these self-deceiving ways of contending with the fear that comes from the recognition of our finitude. The awareness of the inadequacy and shallowness of these responses is the source of the overwhelming sense of guilt of which Paul speaks.

IV

To summarize what I have argued so far: I have suggested that the Christian ethic, and its attendant understanding of human nature, must be interpreted in a way that takes due note of the fact that we are a part of the natural order and are not aliens in it. As far as the injunctions of Christian ethics are concerned, this means that we must recognize that other species have to be included among those we see as our neighbours. What this means in detail is something that we have to work out, just as our duties to our human neighbours have to be worked out and are not self-evident. As the psychologists and sociologists and historians and poets can help to teach us what our human neighbours need, so the experts in ethology, or animal behaviour, can help to teach us how the properly-disposed person should treat members of other species. To be properly disposed is the only ethically-defensible response to the understanding that the natural order that they belong to is the one that our Creator has chosen to use to produce us.

This last recognition means that we can no longer see the sinfulness of our unregenerate natures as a historical consequence of the transgression of our first human ancestors. Many of the components of our natures come down to us as genetic endowments from the long eras before fully human choice was possible. And many of the features of the natural world, including pain and death, preceded humanity and were also inherited by us. So they, too, would seem to be a part of the creative process that has produced us – so that even though we may not like them, we do not have to shoulder the blame for them!

I am not arguing the absurd thesis that humans are 'merely'

animals, or that humanity does not have unique endowments and a unique *calling* in creation. I am merely arguing that human uniqueness consists in having a unique calling among God's creatures, and does not consist in having had a paradisaical past. So the changes in our natures that this unique calling demands are not changes that return the race to where it was, but are changes that are needed to fit human beings for a higher *future*. I am here joining forces with those who see the Christian view of human nature as essentially a forward-looking, or eschatological, view.

I have made a suggestion, which is not novel and is not essential to my general argument, that since the traditional Fall story can no longer stand as history, we can most plausibly see the Christian diagnosis of the darkness and weakness within our natures, which Paul judges to be the result of the invasion of sin, as having come about through the fact that human beings, from the time of the onset of their understanding of their own finitude and mortality, and of their capacity to judge of good and evil, have made the wrong responses to the chronic anxieties that these generate. They have leaned on those inherited capacities for the acquisition of power and security and exclusionary competitiveness, and have elected to combine these with the myriad forms of self-deception that only highly intelligent beings can think up. These are the evil inclinations that each of us inherits and passes on by example. And it is these that the Christian proclamation calls upon us to transcend.

V

If all this is not indigestible enough, a major problem remains. It is not a practical problem, but the sort of theoretical problem that has given thinkers pause for generations. It is the problem of evil in the natural world. The problem of evil is the problem of how it can be that a God whom the Christian proclamation portrays as loving as well as almighty and all-knowing, can permit all the evils that we see around us, and are enjoined by the Christian ethic to combat. The most effective answer to the problem of evil has always been what is known as the Free Will Defence. This is the argument that God created us with a freedom to choose whether to respond to his demands or not, and that freedom cannot exist without a significant degree of power to do what one chooses. The evils in our world are the result of the obvious fact that human beings choose badly, not well; for God to have made these evils impossible, he would have had to create us without the powers that our freedom entails.

This Defence is a powerful one. It does not, however, explain what are called natural evils – that is, such evils as earthquakes and diseases, that human beings do not create. Some thinkers have tried to extend the Free Will Defence to cover them also, by suggesting that some actual natural evils have already to be *there* for us to respond to before we can be morally mature creatures as well as free ones: that the world is, in John Hick's language, a vale of soul-making,[14] so that we are able to respond to the tests life places before us well (that is, with forbearance and fortitude) rather than badly (with self-pity and resentment). For us to have these kinds of choice, which are integral to our development as mature moral agents and servants of God, some actual evils have to be present in our world before we enter it.

This extension of the Free Will Defence is also plausible, given the centrality of certain virtues like compassion and forbearance in the Christian ideal of the redeemed personality. But again, there are many apparent evils that it cannot account for, in particular the suffering and death in the animal realm that preceded the existence of human beings and continues even where it has no connection with human choice. It is here that the traditional Fall story assisted apologists by allowing them to say that these evils were visited on the animal world in consequence of Adam's primal transgression. Since we now know this is not how it was, what are we to say?

I find this a problem of the greatest difficulty, but I must address it as best I can. Earlier I referred to a quotation from *The Montreal Declaration of Anglican Essentials*, that declares that 'The almighty triune God created a universe that was in every way good until creaturely rebellion disrupted it.' I made a passing suggestion that if we reject the traditional doctrine of the Fall we perhaps might say that the natural world into which humanity came was indeed 'in every way good' when we arrived, even though it was not the paradise that the traditional doctrine says it was. At the risk of straining patience and credulity, I want to end by suggesting that the Christian has, in the light of our modern knowledge, to contemplate making something close to this very judgment.

To make it a little less unpalatable to consider it, I would like to make two preliminary points. First, the natural order, with all its destruction and death, has been the process that our Creator has used, or permitted, in order to produce *us*.

95

In these circumstances, it behoves us to acknowledge that it cannot be all bad. More seriously, perhaps, if Christians are right to adopt some of the main objectives of preservationism, and to judge it their duty to restore as much of nature as possible to its pre-human condition, this implies a positive evaluation of that pre-human condition. Of course, if I think it my duty to leave Nature alone to its own ways, that does not imply I judge it to be perfect; only that I do not presume to think I can improve on it even if I have power to alter it. But its evaluative implications are clearly positive ones.

To pass beyond these preliminaries, I want to look at the scriptural texts that are sometimes invoked when ecological matters are discussed, by Christians and their critics. The most commonly mentioned are Genesis 1.26–29, where God gives man dominion over Nature, and Genesis 9.1–7, the so-called covenant with Noah, where he and his descendants are given the animals as well as the plants for food. These texts are often thought, rightly or wrongly, to convey the message that the natural order exists to serve humans and somehow relates to God only through us. A second group of texts are two famous passages in Isaiah, embodying the vision of a whole new world in which the conflicts endemic in Nature have passed away; the first is Isaiah 11.1–9, the second is Isaiah 65.17–25, which tells us the wolf and the lamb will feed together, and the lion will eat straw like the ox. 'They shall not hurt or destroy on all my holy mountain, says the Lord'. To these two texts we should add the famous statement of Paul in Romans 8.18–25, where he says the whole universe groans in all its parts and awaits deliverance. These texts are traditionally read as telling us that just as the denizens of the natural world have suffered the effects of the Fall, so they will share in the benefits of redemption through Christ. One impressive example of this reading is John Wesley's great sermon on 'The General Deliverance'.[15]

But in addition to these two groups of texts, there is another, much lengthier, scriptural passage that is oddly left out of consideration in most of the discussions I have read. I refer to chapters 38 to 41 of the book of Job. The message this conveys is the exact opposite of the message normally read into the Genesis texts. Job, it will be recalled, has been demanding an accounting for his sufferings, which, contrary to the opinion of his friends, he insists he has not deserved. The answer he gets from the Lord is not what he demands, yet it reduces him to repentance. The content of this answer is a mighty hymn to the glories of creation – to the forces of inanimate Nature, and to the prowess of the ostrich and the hawk and the vulture and the whale (or perhaps it is the hippopotamus) and the crocodile and other creatures that man has had no hand in creating and in which the Lord clearly delights – whether man does or not. The message is that Job, and of course the rest of us, are not the only ones with claims to the Lord's attention, or the only ones whose nature and fortunes concern him. The crocodile's very fierceness, and his very grotesqueness, both features that have no positive value for humans, do have such value for God.

I am surprised that this passage is not invoked more often, if at all, in environmental debates; because its message is the very one that preservationists carry out when they try to retain wilderness and the species they find in it. I think of those in my own province of Alberta, Canada, who have tried to reintroduce the swift fox to the prairies; of US naturalists who have braved the ire of ranchers in order to restore a wolf population to Yellowstone National Park; and

I think of my own university's pleasure in being the nesting-place of a brood of peregrine falcons. These are all, be it noted, predators, and predation causes bloodshed, death, suffering and fear; yet we deplore situations in which herbivorous species like rabbits are permitted to proliferate without risk of serious predation, as they have done in Australia. Why do we hold back from saying that endangered predatory species should be allowed to die out because they cause bloodshed, death and suffering; why do we not suppose that everyone who shoots one of them is doing the Lord's work? If the economy of Nature were left to us, wouldn't we have made it gentler? I suggest that the world in which the fittest survive is the world that manifests the Lord's creative plan (that at least is what *this* text says); that it is because it has been like it is that we have emerged from it; and that in trying to preserve as much of it as we can in its pristine state we are recognizing this. I cannot bring myself to say that it is perfect the way it is; even if I were inclined to, it is hard to use this term of a world that is in such continual and unending change. But at the very least I find it impossible to say that the natural order as it is is inferior, or further from perfection, than the quaint pictures of the Peaceable Kingdom that have been supposed to represent the way it was before human sin allegedly corrupted it.

The book of Job is a pre-Christian text (as are Genesis and Isaiah); but perhaps we should not see the New Testament as superseding its vision of Nature – even though it does indeed supersede its view of human suffering. Certainly the New Testament prevents us, if we pay heed to it, from supposing that we have the right to imitate the predators when necessity does not drive us to it. We are no doubt entitled to take from Nature; but I suggest our Christian duty to it is to leave it alone as far as we can and to restore to it what human activity has deprived it of, as far as we can. Not to tame it, or turn it into a garden, though Christian love can indeed find expression in our own, human-dominated parts of the world, in having tame animals and tending gardens.

I suggest, then, that when the Christian ethic is seen as accommodating a proper acceptance of the need to see other species as our cosmic neighbours, we are better able to absorb the implications of what Darwin has forced us to recognize about our origins: that whether we fully understand it or not, he has shown us the manner in which the creative process that produced us has worked. In such a world, we must see human nature as called to another, and no doubt higher, mode of being than the one from which we have emerged, but that the one from which we have emerged is all around us, and it has its own rights.

The opening of Mark's Gospel tells us that before his ministry Jesus was sent by the Spirit into the wilderness, where he lived among the wild beasts. It has been suggested that this statement is a sign that his ministry heals the enmity between beasts and humans and points to the redemption of both. This may be so. I would certainly judge that it tells us that we who live in a world where we are the threat to the beasts more than they are a threat to us, should try to co-exist with them without enmity. If it is indeed also true that the General Deliverance of which Wesley spoke embraces not only the human world but also the animal world, including the millions of beasts who have already suffered and died as well as those who will be here when the Kingdom arrives, I must confess that this is something whose full import I do not profess to understand, and perhaps it is not even my business.

Notes

Full details on books and articles mentioned in these notes will be found in the bibliography.

1. *What is the Christian Ethic?*

1. 'Lastly, those are not to be tolerated who deny the being of God. Promises, covenants, and oaths, which are the bonds of human society, can have no hold upon an atheist. The taking away of God, though but even in thought, dissolves all.' John Locke, *Letter concerning Toleration*, 47.

2. Joseph Butler, Bishop of Durham, lived from 1692 to 1752. Brief accounts of his thought can be found in the encyclopedia articles on him by Elmer Sprague and R. G. Frey; a more detailed account of his ethics and theology is in Terence Penelhum, *Butler*.

3. This dialogue can be found in all collected translations of Plato. It is frequently included with the *Apology*, *Crito* and *Phaedo*, the four together presenting us with Plato's depiction of the trial and death of Socrates. See, for example, the translation by Hugh Tredennick in Plato, *The Last Days of Socrates*. The fullest edition of the *Euthyphro* itself is that of R. E. Allen, *Plato's Euthyphro and the Earlier Theory of Forms*. For a spirited defence of Euthyphro against the majority philosophical judgment in favour of Socrates, see Peter Geach, 'The Moral Law and the Law of God', in his *God and the Soul*.

4. For example, P. H. Nowell-Smith, 'Morality: Religious and Secular', in Ian T. Ramsey (ed.), *Christian Ethics and Contemporary Philosophy*, pp. 95–112.

5. The literature on this theme is enormous, and I cannot pose as a guide to it. I will merely list a number of works which I have found of particular help, and think that others may. On the general question of what is known about the life and preaching of Jesus, a splendid introduction is Ed Sanders, *The Historical Figure of Jesus*. Paul Ramsey, *Basic Christian Ethics* is a standard work on its subject. I much admire L. H. Marshall, *The Challenge of New Testament Ethics*. See also Oscar Cullmann, *Jesus and the Revolutionaries*, N. T. Wright, *Jesus and the Victory of God*, and the volume *Basileia* edited by Karl Ludwig Schmidt et al. in the Bible Key Words series.

6. On this see Marshall, *The Challenge of New Testament Ethics*, pp. 185–96.

7. See Paul Gooch, *Reflections on Jesus and Socrates*, chapter 2.

8. See the first chapter of Kant's *Groundwork of the Metaphysics of Morals*, e.g. in the English translation by H. J. Paton entitled *The Moral Law*.

2. *Human Nature and its Needs – the Christian Diagnosis*

1. A desire that has some other desire as its object in this way is one that philosophers call a second-order desire. While the recognition of conflicts within the soul, and the need for their proper resolution as a condition of moral development is at least as old as Plato in Book IV of the *Republic*, this particular vocabulary, and the attendant concept of the externality or internality of desires, is very recent. It is due to the work of Harry Frankfurt; see especially his essays 'Freedom of the Will and the Concept of a Person' and 'Identification and Externality', collected with others in *The Importance of What We Care About*. My own position on these questions, which was developed in response to some of his arguments, was worked out in more detail than I have been able to go into here, in an essay entitled 'Human Nature and External Desires'.

2. Thomas Heywood, *A Woman Killed with Kindness*, Scene iii.

3. The claim that someone has taken up a practice or way of life

that frustrates his or her real nature often carries with it an implied prediction that that real nature will somehow break through and reassert itself, by causing a breakdown of some kind. This sort of prediction may well persist in spite of all the evidence that the person is quite settled and happy in the way of life that has been chosen.

4. Romans 7.14–25.

5. The full text, in Romans 5.12–14, is: 'Therefore, just as sin came into the world through one man, and death came through sin, and so death spread to all because all have sinned – sin was indeed in the world before the law, but sin is not reckoned when there is no law. Yet death exercised dominion from Adam to Moses, even over those whose sins were not like the transgression of Adam, who is a type of the one who was to come.'

6. I leave out here the fact that Paul also says that one effect of the promptings of the law on his sinful condition is to increase temptation – to make one inclined to do wrong things just because the law forbids them. This is sin's revenge on conscience.

7. For example, Galatians 2.19b–20a: 'I have been crucified with Christ; and it is no longer I who live, but it is Christ who lives in me'. See also I Corinthians 15.10. For a shrewd and original discussion of these questions, see William Alston, 'The Indwelling of the Holy Spirit', in his volume *Divine Nature and Human Language*. An excellent work on Paul's thought is C. H. Dodd, *The Meaning of Paul for Today*.

8. 'So far from self-love being a natural ordinance of God in nature, it is a devilish perversion. That which in all things only seeks its own, is thereby closed against God. But when through faith man becomes open to God, the love from on high obtains a free course to and through him. He becomes a "tube", by which faith receives everything from God's love and then allows the Divine love to stream out over the world.' Anders Nygren, *Agape and Eros*, pp. 740–1.

9. See D. M. Baillie, *God Was in Christ*, pp. 114ff.

10. I have written a brief account of the Christian teaching in a chapter of Harold Coward (ed.), *Life After Death in World Religions*.

Notes

11. The classic work of scholarship on the early history of these disputes is N. P. Williams, *The Ideas of the Fall and of Original Sin*. The most important and influential modern treatise on the place of sin in human nature is Reinhold Niebuhr, *The Nature and Destiny of Man*. What I say in these pages is at odds with positions taken up in both works (as they are at odds with each other!), but both are indispensable to the serious student of these themes.

12. An important recent treatment of these questions is Richard Swinburne, *Responsibilty and Atonement*.

3. *The Pluralist Challenge*

1. Richard Swinburne, *The Existence of God*.

2. Hume's writings on religion are conveniently collected, and well edited, in J. C. A. Gaskin (ed.), *Dialogues Concerning Natural Religion and The Natural History of Religion*. Kant's views are difficult to disentangle from his wider theory of knowledge, but are to be found in the Transcendental Dialectic of the *Critique of Pure Reason* and *Religion Within the Boundaries of Mere Reason*.

3. The following account is an informal summation of positions found in several works by Alvin Plantinga, especially 'Reason and Belief in God', in Alvin Plantinga and Nicholas Wolterstorff (eds), *Faith and Rationality*, and (more briefly) 'Reformed Epistemology', in Philip L. Quinn and Charles Taliaferro (eds), *A Companion to Philosophy of Religion*. The best-argued statement of the view I summarize (and one that confronts the difficulties with care and candour) is William Alston, *Perceiving God*. I have attempted an assessment of these arguments in more detail in *Reason and Religious Faith* and the essay 'The Idea of Reason', in Peter Byrne and Leslie Houlden (eds), *Companion Encyclopedia of Theology*.

4. The Sceptical tradition in philosophy has been receiving a good deal of scholarly attention recently. See Myles Burnyeat (ed.), *The Skeptical Tradition*.

5. For a general work of high scholarly and philosophical merit that describes the variety of the religions of the world, see Ninian Smart, *The World's Religions*. Harold Coward, *Pluralism: Challenge to World Religions* is a valuable guide to the ways in which the major faiths respond to one another. What I have, following many others, called the pluralist challenge, is usually expressed in terms of what Hick calls the distinction between pre-axial and post-axial religion, the former being 'centrally (but not solely) concerned with the preservation of cosmic and social order' and the latter being 'centrally (but not solely) concerned with the quest for salvation or liberation' (Hick, *An Interpretation of Religion*, p. 22). The major faiths whose apparent incompatibility poses the pluralist challenge are all, of course, of the latter variety.

6. Karl Rahner, 'Christianity and the Non-Christian Religions', in John Hick and Brian Hebblethwaite (eds), *Christianity and Other Religions*.

7. The most important of John Hick's studies on pluralism is *An Interpretation of Religion*. In this chapter I have also given special attention to arguments in *Problems of Religious Pluralism* and *Death and Eternal Life*.

8. For a variety of philosophical and theological assessments of Hick's work, see Arvind Sharma (ed.), *God, Truth and Reality*, and the special issue of the journal *Faith and Philosophy* devoted to pluralism, and edited by Hick himself.

9. Donald M. Baillie, *God Was in Christ*, and Geoffrey Lampe, *God as Spirit*. For Hick's views see essay 4 in *Problems of Religious Pluralism* and 'Jesus and the World Religions', in John Hick (ed.), *The Myth of God Incarnate*. For a recent collection of contributions on this topic by writers of a generally pluralist persuasion, see Leonard Swidler and Paul Mojzes (eds), *The Uniqueness of Jesus*.

10. Hick's discussions of this concept in *Death and Eternal Life* are very valuable. For a recent attempt to show it can be incorporated into Christianity, see Geddes MacGregor, *The Christening of Karma*.

11. For a fine scholarly account of these differing schools, see Ninian Smart, *Doctrine and Argument in Indian Philosophy*.

Notes

12. The finest single essay I know about Socrates is Gregory Vlastos, 'The Paradox of Socrates', in Gregory Vlastos (ed.), *The Philosophy of Socrates*. Christian readers especially will profit from Paul Gooch, *Reflections on Jesus and Socrates*.

13. I must point out (though I can do no more here) that the eschatology outlined in Hick, *Death and Eternal Life*, is developed in a way designed to respond to this difficulty. The core of Hick's response is the distinction between eschatology (the doctrine of the last things) and pareschatology (the doctrine of the next-to-last things), the enlightenment faiths possessing the core of the former and the prophetic faiths the latter.

14. Terence Penelhum, *Reason and Religious Faith*.

4. Humans and the Natural World

1. For two very different accounts of this famous confrontation, see Giorgio De Santillana, *The Crime of Galileo* and Arthur Koestler, *The Sleepwalkers*.

2. Pascal, *Pensées* 116. I quote from the Krailsheimer translation. There is a very large literature on Pascal. Two helpful recent works are Roger Hazelton, *Blaise Pascal: The Genius of His Thought* and Thomas V. Morris, *Making Sense of It All: Pascal and the Meaning of Life*.

3. The literature on evolution is endless. Two volumes that do an excellent job of making clear how foolish it is to contest the fact of evolution and how important it is to try to take the measure of its importance for understanding human nature, are Michael Ruse, *Taking Darwin Seriously*, and Mary Midgley, *Beast and Man*. For a specifically Christian perspective one might begin with William Hasker, 'Theism and Evolutionary Biology', in Philip C. Quinn and Charles Taliaferro, *A Companion to Philosophy of Religion*.

4. *The Montreal Declaration of Anglican Essentials*, item 2.

5. Mark 5.1–13.

6. Revelation 12.9.

7. For a brief account of the Manichean tradition, which at one stage before his Christian conversion had St Augustine among

its adherents, see Ninian Smart, *The World's Religions*, pp. 226–7. The relevant feature of it for the present purpose is the fact that it seems to give near-equal creative power to the Father of Light and the Prince of Darkness.

8. A notable exception to the general reticence of Christian thinkers to extend their ethical thinking in this way is Stephen Clark. See *The Moral Status of Animals*, and his article 'Environmental Ethics', in Peter Byrne and Leslie Houlden, *Companion Encyclopedia of Theology*. A more popular work that connects Christianity and ecological movements is Tim Cooper, *Green Christianity*. A recent collection of essays by Christian writers, Andrew Linzey and Dorothy Yamamoto (eds), *Animals on the Agenda*, is to be warmly commended.

9. John Passmore, *Man's Responsibility for Nature*, p. 101.

10. Arne Naess, 'The Shallow and the Deep, Long-Range Ecology Movement'.

11. See Niebuhr, *The Nature and Destiny of Man*, Vol. 1, chapter 7.

12. C. S. Lewis, *The Problem of Pain*, chapter 9.

13. E. L. Mascall, *The Importance of Being Human*, p. 72.

14. John Hick, *Evil and the God of Love*.

15. *The Works of John Wesley*, Vol. 2, Sermon 60.

Bibliography

Allen, R. E., *Plato's Euthyphro and the Earlier Theory of Forms*, New York: Humanities Press 1970.

Alston, William P., *Divine Nature and Human Language*, Ithaca: Cornell University Press 1989.

——, *Perceiving God*, Ithaca: Cornell University Press 1991.

Baillie, D. M., *God Was in Christ*, 2nd edn., London: Faber & Faber 1955.

Burnyeat, Myles (ed.), *The Skeptical Tradition*, Berkeley and Los Angeles: University of California Press 1983.

Butler, Joseph, *The Works of Joseph Butler*, ed. J. H. Bernard, Vol. 1., London: Macmillan 1900.

Byrne, Peter, and Houlden, Leslie (eds), *Companion Encyclopedia of Theology*, London: Routledge 1995.

Clark, Stephen R. L., *The Moral Status of Animals*, Oxford: Clarendon Press 1977.

Cooper, Tim, *Green Christianity*, London: Hodder & Stoughton, 1990.

Coward, Harold, *Pluralism: Challenge to World Religions*, Maryknoll, NY: Orbis Books 1985.

Coward, Harold (ed.), *Life After Death in World Religions*, Maryknoll, NY: Orbis Books 1997.

Cullmann, Oscar, *Jesus and the Revolutionaries*, New York: Harper & Row 1970.

De Santillana, Giorgio, *The Crime of Galileo*, Chicago: University of Chicago Press 1955.

Dodd, C. H., *The Meaning of Paul for Today*, New York: Meridian Books 1957.

Forster, E. M., *Maurice*, Toronto: Macmillan 1971.

Bibliography

Frankfurt, Harry G., *The Importance of What We Care About*, Cambridge: Cambridge University Press 1988.

Frey, R. G., 'Butler', in *Routledge Encyclopedia of Philosophy*, Vol. 2, London: Routledge 1998.

Geach, Peter, *God and the Soul*, London: Routledge 1969.

Gooch, Paul, *Reflections on Jesus and Socrates*, New Haven: Yale University Press 1996.

Hazelton, Roger, *Blaise Pascal: The Genius of His Thought*, Philadelphia: Westminster Press 1974.

Heywood, Thomas, *A Woman Killed with Kindness*, ed. R. W. Van Fossen, London: Methuen 1961.

Hick, John, *Death and Eternal Life*, London: Collins 1976.

——, *Evil and the God of Love*, London: Macmillan 1966.

——, *An Interpretation of Religion*, Houndmills, Basingstoke: Macmillan Press 1989.

——, *Problems of Religious Pluralism*, Houndmills, Basingstoke: Macmillan Press 1985.

Hick, John (ed.), special issue, 'Religious Pluralism', *Faith and Philosophy*, Vol. 5, Number 4, 1988.

——, *The Myth of God Incarnate*, London: SCM Press, 1977.

Hick, John and Brian Hebblethwaite (eds), *Christianity and Other Religions*, London: Collins 1980.

Hume, David, *Dialogues Concerning Natural Religion and The Natural History of Religion*, ed. J. C. A. Gaskin (World's Classics), Oxford: Oxford University Press 1993.

Kant, Immanuel, *Critique of Pure Reason*, trans. Norman Kemp Smith, London: Macmillan 1950.

——, *Religion Within the Boundaries of Mere Reason*, trans. Allen Wood and George di Giovanni, Cambridge: Cambridge University Press 1998.

Koestler, Arthur, *The Sleepwalkers*, London: Hutchinson 1968.

Lampe, G. W. H., *God as Spirit*, Oxford: Clarendon Press 1977.

Linzey, Andrew and Yamamoto, Dorothy (eds), *Animals on the Agenda*, London: SCM Press 1998.

Lewis, C. S., *The Problem of Pain*, 1940, repr. New York: Macmillan 1962.

Locke, John, *The Works of John Locke*, Vol. 6, London: Thomas

Bibliography

Tegg et al. 1823, repr. Scientia Verlag Aalen, Germany 1963.

Marshall, L. H., *The Challenge of New Testament Ethics*, London: Macmillan 1947.

MacGregor, Geddes, *The Christening of Karma*, Wheaton, IL: Theosophical Publishing House 1984.

Mascall, E. L., *The Importance of Being Human*, London: Oxford University Press 1959.

Midgley, Mary, *Beast and Man*, London: Methuen 1980.

The Montreal Declaration of Anglican Essentials, 21 June 1994, Montreal.

Morris, Thomas V., *Making Sense of It All: Pascal and the Meaning of Life*, Grand Rapids, MI: Eerdmans 1992.

Niebuhr, Reinhold, *The Nature and Destiny of Man*, London: Nisbet 1941.

Naess, Arne, 'The Shallow and the Deep, Long-Range Ecology Movement', *Inquiry* 16, 1973.

Nygren, Anders, *Agape and Eros*, trans. Philip S. Watson, New York: Harper & Row 1969.

Pascal, Blaise, *Pensées*, trans. A. J. Krailsheimer, Harmondsworth: Penguin 1966.

Passmore, John, *Man's Responsibility for Nature*, 2nd edn., London: Duckworth 1980.

Paton, H. J. (ed. and trans.), *The Moral Law or Kant's Groundwork of the Metaphysic of Morals*, London: Hutchinson 1947.

Penelhum, Terence, *Butler*, London: Routledge 1985.

——, 'Human Nature and External Desires', *The Monist* 62, 1979.

——, *Reason and Religious Faith*, Boulder, CO: Westview Press 1995.

Plantinga, Alvin, and Wolterstorff, Nicholas (eds), *Faith and Rationality*, Notre Dame: University of Notre Dame Press 1983.

Plato, *The Last Days of Socrates*, trans. Hugh Tredennick, Harmondsworth: Penguin 1954.

——, *The Republic of Plato*, trans. F. M. Cornford, Oxford: Clarendon Press 1941.

Quinn, Philip L. and Taliaferro Charles (eds), *A Companion to Philosophy of Religion*, Oxford: Blackwell 1997.

Bibliography

Ramsey, Ian T., *Christian Ethics and Contemporary Philosophy*, London: SCM Press 1966.

Ramsey, Paul, *Basic Christian Ethics*, Chicago: University of Chicago Press 1950.

Ruse, Michael, *Taking Darwin Seriously*, Amherst, NY: Prometheus Books 1998.

Sanders, E. P. T*he Historical Figure of Jesus*, Harmondsworth: Penguin 1993.

Schmidt, K. L. et al. (eds), *Basileia* (Bible Key Words Series), London: Adam & Charles Black 1957.

Sharma, Arvind (ed.), *God, Truth and Reality: Essays in Honour of John Hick*, New York: St Martin's Press 1993.

Smart, Ninian, *Doctrine and Argument in Indian Philosophy*, London: Allen & Unwin 1964.

——, *The World's Religions*. 2nd edn., Cambridge: Cambridge University Press 1998.

Sprague, Elmer, 'Butler, Joseph', in *Encyclopedia of Philosophy*, Vol. 1, New York: The Macmillan Company and the Free Press 1967.

Stump, Eleonore (ed.), *Reasoned Faith*, Ithaca: Cornell University Press 1993.

Swidler, Leonard and Mojzes, Paul (eds), *The Uniqueness of Jesus*, Maryknoll, NY: Orbis Books 1997.

Swinburne, Richard, *The Existence of God*, Oxford: Clarendon Press 1979.

——, *Responsibility and Atonement*, Oxford: Clarendon Press 1989.

Van Inwagen, Peter, *God, Knowledge and Mystery*, Ithaca: Cornell University Press 1995.

Vlastos, Gregory (ed.), *The Philosophy of Socrates*, Garden City, NY: Doubleday 1971.

Wesley, John, *The Works of John Wesley*, Vol. 2, ed. Albert C. Outler, Nashville: Abingdon Press, 1985.

Williams, Norman Powell, *The Ideas of the Fall and of Original Sin*, London: Longmans, Green 1927.

Wright, N. T. *Jesus and the Victory of God*, London: SPCK and Minneapolis: Fortress Press 1996.

General Index

General Index

General Index

Index of Biblical References